DISCOURSES
Books 3 and 4

DISCOURSES
Books 3 and 4

EPICTETUS

English translation by
P. E. Matheson

DOVER PUBLICATIONS, INC.
Mineola, New York

DOVER PHILOSOPHICAL CLASSICS

Bibliographical Note

This Dover edition, first published in 2004, is an unabridged republication of Books Three and Four of *The Discourses*, from *Epictetus: The Discourses and Manual*, translated by P. E. Matheson and originally published by The Clarendon Press, Oxford, in 1916. In this edition we have Americanized the translator's spelling and punctuation, and have incorporated into the footnotes all the relevant information from the Oxford edition's Glossary of Names.

Library of Congress Cataloging-in-Publication Data

Epictetus.
   [Discourses. Book 3–4. English]
   Discourses. Books 3 and 4 / Epictetus ; English translation by P.E. Matheson.
      p. cm. — (Dover philosophical classics)
   Originally published: 1916.
   ISBN 0-486-43443-5 (pbk.)
   1. Stoics. I. Matheson, P. E. (Percy Ewing), 1859–1946. II. Title. III. Series.

B561.D52E5 2004
188—dc22

2004041390

Manufactured in the United States of America
Dover Publications, Inc., 31 East 2nd Street, Mineola, N.Y. 11501

Contents

Discourses: Book Three

Chapter 1. On Adornment — 1
Chapter 2. (1) In what matters should the man who is to make progress train himself: and (2) That we neglect what is most vital — 6
Chapter 3. What is the material with which the good man deals: and what should be the object of our training — 8
Chapter 4. Against one who was indecorously excited in the theater — 10
Chapter 5. Against those who make illness an excuse for leaving the lecture-room — 11
Chapter 6. Scattered sayings — 13
Chapter 7. Dialogue with the Commissioner of the Free Cities, who was an Epicurean — 14
Chapter 8. How we should train ourselves to deal with impressions — 17
Chapter 9. To a Rhetor going up to Rome for a trial — 18
Chapter 10. How one should bear illnesses — 20
Chapter 11. Scattered sayings — 22
Chapter 12. On training — 22
Chapter 13. What a "forlorn" condition means, and a "forlorn" man — 24
Chapter 14. Scattered sayings — 26
Chapter 15. That we should approach everything with consideration — 27
Chapter 16. That we must be cautious in our social relations — 29
Chapter 17. Concerning Providence — 30
Chapter 18. That we must not allow news to disturb us — 31
Chapter 19. What is the difference between the philosopher and the uneducated man — 32

Chapter 20. That benefit may be derived from all outward things	32
Chapter 21. To those who undertake the profession of teacher with a light heart	34
Chapter 22. On the calling of the Cynic	36
Chapter 23. To those who read and discourse for display	46
Chapter 24. That we ought not to spend our feelings on things beyond our power	51
Chapter 25. To those who fail to achieve what they set before them	61
Chapter 26. To those who fear want	62

Discourses: Book Four

Chapter 1. On Freedom	67
Chapter 2. On intercourse with men	85
Chapter 3. What to aim at in exchange	86
Chapter 4. To those whose heart is set on a quiet life	87
Chapter 5. To those that are contentious and brutal	92
Chapter 6. To those who are distressed at being pitied	95
Chapter 7. On freedom from fear	99
Chapter 8. To those who hastily assume the character of Philosophers	104
Chapter 9. To one who was modest and has become shameless	108
Chapter 10. What things we should despise, and what we should deem important	109
Chapter 11. On cleanliness	112
Chapter 12. On attention	116
Chapter 13. To those who lightly communicate their secrets	117

BOOK THREE

CHAPTER 1: On Adornment

When a young student of rhetoric came into his lecture-room with his hair elaborately arranged and paying great attention to his dress in general: Tell me, said he, do you not think that some dogs and horses are beautiful and some ugly, and is it not so with every creature?

"I think so," he said.

Is not the same true of men, some are beautiful, some ugly?

"Certainly."

Now do we give the attribute "beautiful" to each of them in their own kind on the same grounds or on special grounds in each case? Listen and you will see what I mean. Since we see that a dog is born for one thing and a horse for another, and a nightingale, if you like to take that, for another, speaking generally one would not be giving an absurd opinion in saying that each of them was beautiful when it best fulfilled its nature; and since the nature of each is different, I think that each of them would be beautiful in a different way, would it not?

"Yes."

So that what makes a dog beautiful makes a horse ugly, and what makes a horse beautiful makes a dog ugly, seeing that their natures are different?

"So it seems."

Yes, for what makes a pancratiast beautiful does not, I imagine, make a good wrestler, and makes a very ridiculous runner; and one who is beautiful for the pentathlon makes a very ugly appearance as a wrestler?[1]

"True," he said.

---

[1] The *pancration* consisted of boxing and wrestling, and was supposed to test all a man's powers. The *pentathlon* included running, jumping, quoit-throwing, spear-throwing, and wrestling.

What then makes a man beautiful if it is not that which in its kind makes dog and horse beautiful?

"It is just that," he said.

What then makes a dog beautiful? The presence of a dog's virtue. What makes a horse beautiful? The presence of a horse's virtue. What makes a man beautiful? Is it the presence of a man's virtue? Therefore, young man, if you would be beautiful, make this the object of your effort, human virtue. And what is human virtue? Consider whom you praise, when you praise men dispassionately; do you praise the just or the unjust?

"The just."

Do you praise the temperate or the intemperate?

"The temperate."

The continent or the incontinent?

"The continent."

Therefore if you make yourself such an one, be sure that you will make yourself beautiful, but as long as you neglect this you cannot help being ugly, though you should use every device to appear beautiful.

But beyond this I do not know what more to say to you; for, if I say what I think, I shall vex you and you will go out and perhaps never return, but if I say nothing, consider what my conduct will be then; you come to me to get good, and I shall be refusing to do you good; you come to me to consult a philosopher, and I shall be refusing you a philosopher's advice. Besides, it is cruelty towards you to leave you uncorrected. If some day hereafter you come to your senses you will accuse me with good reason: "What did Epictetus find in me, that when he saw me coming in to him in such a shameful state he should do nothing for me and say never a word to me? Did he so utterly despair of me? Was I not young? Was I not fit to listen to discourse? How many other young men make many mistakes like me in their youth? I hear that one Polemo,[2] who had been the most intemperate of young men, underwent such a wonderful change. Grant that he did not think I should be a Polemo: he could have set my hair right, have taken away my bangles, have stopped me pulling my hairs out, but seeing that I had the aspect of—whom shall I say?[3]—he said nothing." I do not say whose aspect this is, but you will say it for yourself when you come to look into your own heart, and you will learn what it means and what sort of men they are who adopt it.

---

[2] A young profligate converted to the philosophic life by Xenocrates; head of the Academy, c. 314–273 B.C.

[3] The suggestion is that the pupil comes to Epictetus looking like a profligate.

Book Three

If hereafter you bring this charge against me, what defense shall I be able to make?

Yes, but suppose I do speak, and he will not obey?

Did Laius[4] obey Apollo? Did he not go away in his drunken stupor and dismiss the oracle from his mind? What then? Did Apollo withhold the truth from him for that reason? Indeed I do not know whether you will obey me or not, but Apollo knew most certainly that Laius would not obey, and yet he spoke. Why did he speak? Nay, why is he Apollo, why does he give oracles, why has he set himself in this position, to be a Prophet and a Fountain of truth, so that men from all the world come to him? Why is "Know thyself" written up over his shrine, though no one understands it?

Did Socrates persuade all who came to him to attend to their characters? Not one in a thousand! Nevertheless when appointed to this post, as he says, by the ordinance of God, he refused to desert it. Nay, what did he say to his judges? "If you acquit me," he says, "on these terms, that I cease to do what I do now, I shall not accept your offer, nor give up my ways, but I shall go to any one I meet, young or old, and put to him these questions that I put now, and I shall question you my fellow citizens far more than any other because you are nearer akin to me."

Are you so fussy and interfering, Socrates? What do you care what we do?

"What language to use! You are my fellow and kinsman, yet you neglect yourself and provide the city with a bad citizen, your kinsmen with a bad kinsman, and your neighbors with a bad neighbor!"

"Who are you, then?"

To this question it is a weighty answer to say, "I am he who is bound to take interest in men." For ordinary cattle dare not resist the lion; but if the bull comes up to withstand him, say to him, if you think fit, "Who are you?" and "What do you care? Man! in every class of creatures nature produces some exceptional specimen; it is so among cattle, dogs, bees, horses. Do not say then to the exception, "What are you then?" If you do, he will get a voice somehow and say, "I am like the purple in a garment: do not require me to be like the rest, nor blame my nature, because it made me different from the rest."

What then? Am I fit to play this part? How can I be? And are you fit to hear the truth? Would that it were so! Nevertheless since I am condemned, it seems, to wear a white beard and a cloak, and since you come to me as to a philosopher, I will not treat you cruelly as though I

---

[4] The father of Oedipus in the Theban legend; he consulted the oracle of Delphi, who warned him that he would kill his son if he begat one.

despaired of you, but will say, Young man, who is it that you want to make beautiful? First get to know who you are and then adorn yourself. You are a man, that is, a mortal creature which has the power to deal with impressions rationally. What does "rationally" mean? Perfectly, and in accordance with nature. What then is your distinctive possession? Your animal nature? No. Your mortality? No. Your power to deal with impressions? No. Your reasoning faculty is the distinctive one: this you must adorn and make beautiful. Leave your hair to Him that formed it in accordance with His will. Tell me, what other names have you? Are you man or woman?

"Man."

Adorn Man then, not Woman. Woman is born smooth and tender, and if she has much hair on her body it is a prodigy, and exhibited in Rome as a prodigy. But in a man it is a prodigy not to be hairy: if he is born smooth it is a prodigy, and if he make himself smooth by shaving and plucking, what are we to make of him? Where are we to show him, and what notice are we to put up? "I will show you a man who prefers to be a woman." What a shocking exhibition! Every one will be astonished at the notice: by Zeus, I think that even the men who pluck out their hairs do so without understanding that this is what they are doing! Man, what complaint have you to make of Nature? Is it that she made you a man? Ought she to have made all to be women? Why, if all were women, there would be no one to adorn yourself for.

If you are not satisfied with your condition as it is, do the thing completely. Remove—what shall I call it?—that which is the cause of your hairiness; make yourself a woman out and out, and not half-man, half-woman, and then we shall not be misled. Whom do you wish to please? Your darling womenkind? Then please them as a man.

"Yes, but they like smooth men."

Go and hang yourself! If they liked unnatural creatures, would you become one? Is this your function, is this what you were born for, that profligate women should take pleasure in you? Is it with this character that we are to make you a citizen of Corinth, and, if it so chance, City-warden, or Governor of the Ephebi,[5] or General, or Steward of the games? Well, and when you have married a wife, are you going to pluck yourself smooth? For whom and for what? And when you have begotten boys, are you going to bring them into our citizenship as plucked creatures too? Noble citizen and senator and orator! Is this the kind of young man we are to pray to have bred and reared for us?

Nay, by the gods, young man! but when once you have heard these

---

[5] These are all local officers in Corinth. The Ephebi were young men of 18–20, under military training.

words, go and say to yourself: "These are not the words of Epictetus: how could they be? but some kind god speaks through him; for it would never have occurred to Epictetus to say this, as he is not wont to speak to any one. Come then, let us obey God, that we may not incur God's wrath."

Why, if a raven croaks and gives you a sign, it is not the raven that gives the sign, but God through him: and if He gives you a sign through a human voice, will He not be making man tell you this, that you may learn the power of the divine, and see that it gives signs to some in this way, and to others in that, and of the highest and most sovereign matters gives signs through the noblest messenger? What else is the meaning of the poet, when he says

> *Since we warned him*
> *By Hermes Argus-slayer, clear of sight,*
> *To slay him not nor woo his wedded wife?*

And as Hermes[6] was sent down to tell him this, so now the gods have sent "Hermes the Argus-slayer, their messenger," and tell you this—not to pervert what is good and right, and not to interfere with it, but to leave man man and woman woman, the beautiful person a beautiful person, and the ugly person an ugly person. For you are not flesh, nor hair, but a rational will: if you get this beautiful, then you will be beautiful.

So far I do not dare to tell you that you are ugly, for I think you would hear anything rather than that. But see what Socrates says to Alcibiades,[7] most beautiful and charming of men: "Strive then to attain beauty." What does he say to him? Does he say, "Arrange your hair and smooth your legs?" God forbid! but "Set your will in order, rid it of bad judgements."

"How treat the poor body then?"

According to its nature: that is God's concern, trust it to Him.

"What then? Is the body to be unclean?"

God forbid! but cleanse your true, natural self: let man be clean as man, woman as woman, child as child.

Nay, let us pluck out the lion's mane,[8] lest it be unclean, and the cock's comb, for he too must be clean!

Clean? yes, but clean as a cock, and the lion as a lion, and the hound of the chase as such a hound should be.

---

[6] The messenger of the gods.
[7] The Athenian statesman, pupil and friend of Socrates.
[8] Epictetus ironically suggests that the student's notion of cleanliness is merely external.

CHAPTER 2: (1) In What Matters Should the Man Who Is to Make Progress Train Himself: and (2) That We Neglect What Is Most Vital

There are three departments in which a man who is to be good and noble must be trained. The first concerns the will to get and will to avoid; he must be trained not to fail to get what he wills to get nor fall into what he wills to avoid. The second is concerned with impulse to act and not to act, and, in a word, the sphere of what is fitting: that we should act in order, with due consideration, and with proper care. The object of the third is that we may not be deceived, and may not judge at random, and generally it is concerned with assent.

Of these the most important and the most pressing is the first, which is concerned with strong emotions, for such emotion does not arise except when the will to get or the will to avoid fails of its object. This it is which brings with it disturbances, tumults, misfortunes, bad fortunes, mournings, lamentations, envies; which makes men envious and jealous—passions which make us unable to listen to reason.

The second is the sphere of what is fitting: for I must not be without feeling like a statue, but must maintain my natural and acquired relations, as a religious man, as son, brother, father, citizen.

The third department is appropriate only for those who are already making progress, and is concerned with giving certainty in the very things we have spoken of, so that even in sleep or drunkenness or melancholy no untested impression may come upon us unawares.

"This," says a pupil, "is beyond us."

But the philosophers of today have disregarded the first and the second departments, and devote themselves to the third—variable premisses, syllogisms concluding with a question, hypothetical syllogisms, fallacious arguments.

"Of course," he says, "when a man is engaged on these subjects he must take pains to escape being deceived." But whose business is it to do this? It is only for the man who is already good.

In logic then you fall short: but have you reached perfection in other subjects? Are you proof against deceit in regard to money? If you see a pretty girl, do you resist the impression? If your neighbor comes in for an inheritance, do you not feel a twinge? Do you lack nothing now but security of judgement? Unhappy man, even while you are learning this lesson you are in an agony of terror lest some one should think scorn of you, and you ask whether any one is talking about you! And if some one comes and tells you, "We were discussing who was the best philosopher, and one who was there said, 'There is only one philosopher, So-and-so (naming you),'" straightway your poor little four-inch soul shoots up to two cubits! Then if another who is by says, "Nonsense! It is not worth while to listen to So-and-so: what does he know? he has the first rudiments, nothing more," you are beside yourself, and grow pale and cry out at once, "I will show him the man I am, he shall see I am a great philosopher." Why, the facts themselves are evidence; why do you want to show it by something else? Do you not know that Diogenes pointed out one of the sophists thus, making a vulgar gesture?[1] Then, when the man was furious, "That is So-and-so," said he, "I have shown him to you." A man is not indeed like a stone or a log, that you can show what he is by just pointing a finger, but you show what he is as a man, when you show what are his judgements.

Let us look at your judgements too. Is it not clear that you set no value on your will, but look outside to things beyond your will?—what So-and-so will say, what men will think of you, whether they will think you a scholar, one who has read Chrysippus or Antipater,[2] for if you have read them and Archedemus[3] as well, you have read everything. Why are you still in an agony, lest you should fail to show us what manner of man you are? Would you like me to say what manner of man you showed yourself to us? A man who comes before us mean, critical, quick-tempered, cowardly, blaming everything, accusing every one, never quiet, vainglorious—that is what you showed us! Go away now and read Archedemus; then if a mouse fall and make a noise, you die of fright! For the same sort of death awaits you, as—whom shall I say?—Crinis![4] He too was proud of understanding Archedemus!

Unhappy man, will you not leave these things alone, which do not concern you? They are suited only to those who can learn them without confusion, to those who are able to say, "I feel no anger, pain, or envy; I am under no hindrance, no constraint. What is left for me to do? I have leisure and peace of mind. Let us see how we ought to deal with logical changes:[5] let us see how one may adopt a hypothesis and not be led to an absurd conclusion."

These are matters well enough for men like that.[6] It is fitting for sailors who are in good trim to light a fire, and take their dinner, if luck serves, and to sing and dance: but you come to me when the ship is sinking and begin hoisting the topsails!

---

[1] Lit., "stretching out the middle finger." This was an obscene gesture.
[2] Antipater of Tarsus, a Stoic, who taught Panaetius, the friend of the Scipios (c. 140 B.C.).
[3] A Stoic of Tarsus, coupled with Antipater by Cicero and Epictetus.
[4] A Stoic philosopher, who wrote on Dialectic.
[5] Lit., "alterations in logical terms or premisses and the like."
[6] *I.e.*, men who are free from passion and tumult of mind.

CHAPTER 3: What Is the Material with Which the Good Man Deals: and What Should Be the Object of Our Training

The material of the good man is his own Governing Principle, as the body is the material of the physician and trainer, the land of the farmer; and it is the function of the good man to deal with his impressions naturally. And just as it is the nature of every soul to assent to what is true and dissent from what is false, and withhold judgement in what is uncertain, so it is its nature to be moved with the will to get what is good and the will to avoid what is evil, and to be neutral towards what is neither good nor evil. For just as neither the banker nor the greengrocer can refuse the Emperor's currency, but, if you show it, he must part, willy-nilly, with what the coin will buy, so it is also with the soul. The very sight of good attracts one towards it, the sight of evil repels. The soul will never reject a clear impression of good, any more than we reject Caesar's currency. On this depends every motion of man and of God. Therefore the good is preferred to every tie of kinship.

I have no concern with my father, but with the good!

"Are you so hard-hearted?"

It is my nature; this is the currency which God has given me. Therefore if the good is different from the noble and just, then father and brother, country and all such things disappear.

I say, am I to neglect my good, that you may get it? am I to make way for you? Why should I?

"I am your father."

But not my good.

"I am your brother."

But not my good. If we make the good consist in right will, the mere maintenance of such relations[1] becomes good: further, he who resigns some of his external possessions attains the good.

"My father is taking away my money."

But he is not harming you.

"My brother will have the greater part of the land."

Let him have as much as he likes: does he gain in character? Is he more modest, trustworthy, brotherly? Who can eject one from *that* possession? Not even Zeus: nor did He wish to eject me; He put my character in my keeping and gave it me as He had it himself, unhindered, unfettered, unrestrained.

Inasmuch then as different people have a different currency, a man shows his coin and gets what it will buy. A thief has come to the

---

[1] *I.e.*, relations with father, brother, etc.

province as Proconsul. What coin does he use? Money. Show him money, and carry off what you will. An adulterer has come. What currency does he use? Pretty girls. "Take your coin," says he, "and sell me the thing I want." Give, and buy. Another's heart is set on minions. Give him the coin and take what you will. Another is a sportsman. Give him a fine horse or dog. With sighs and groans he will sell you what you like for it: for he is constrained from within, by Another, who has ordained this currency.[2]

It is by this principle above all that you must guide yourself in training. Go out as soon as it is dawn and whomsoever you may see and hear, question yourself and answer as to an interrogator.

What did you see? A beautiful woman or boy. Apply the rule: Is this within the will's control or beyond it? Beyond. Away with it then!

What did you see? One mourning at his child's death. Apply the rule. Is death beyond the will, or can the will control it? Death is beyond the will's control. Put it out of the way then!

Did a Consul meet you? Apply the rule. What is a consulship? Is it beyond the will's control or within it? Beyond it. Take it away: the coin will not pass; reject it, you have no concern with it.

I say, if we did this and trained ourselves on this principle every day from dawn to night, we should indeed achieve something. As it is, we are caught open-mouthed by every impression we meet, and only in the lecture-room, if then, does our mind wake up a little. Then we go into the street and if we see a mourner we say, "He is undone"; if a Consul, "Lucky man"; if an outlaw, "Miserable man"; if a poor man, "Wretched man, he has nothing to buy food with."

These mistaken judgements we must eradicate, and concentrate our efforts on doing so. For what is weeping and lamenting? A matter of judgement. What is misfortune? Judgement. What is faction, discord, criticism, accusation, irreligion, foolishness? All these are judgements, nothing else, and judgements passed on things beyond the will, as though they were good and evil. Only let a man turn these efforts to the sphere of the will, and I guarantee that he will enjoy peace of mind, whatever his circumstances may be.

The soul is like a dish full of water, and the impressions like the rays of light which strike the water. Now when the water is disturbed the light seems to be disturbed too, but it is not really disturbed. So when a man has a fit of dizziness, the arts and virtues are not put to confu-

---

[2] Lit., "Another constrains him," *i.e.*, God. God has ordained that man should put first whatever he regards as his "good": the choice of his "good" depends on himself.

sion, but only the spirit[3] in which they exist: when this is at rest, they come to rest too.

CHAPTER 4: Against One Who Was Indecorously Excited in the THEATER

When the Procurator of Epirus[1] offended decorum by the way he showed interest in a comedian, the people reviled him for this; thereupon when he brought word of this to Epictetus and expressed annoyance at those who reviled him: Why! he said, what harm were they doing? They too showed their interest as you did!

"What!" said he, "is this the way they show interest?"

Yes, he said, when they saw you, their Governor, the friend and Procurator of Caesar, showing your interest in this way, would you not expect them to do the same? If it is not right to show interest in that way, leave off doing it yourself: but if it is right, why are you angry at their imitating you? For whom else but you, their superiors, have the people to imitate? Whom are they to look to when they come to the theater but you? "See," they say, "how Caesar's Procurator behaves in the theater. He cries out: then I will cry out too. He jumps from his seat, I will do so too. His claque of slaves shout from their scattered seats: I have no slaves, I will cry as loud as I can to make up for it." You ought to know then that when you enter the theater you enter it as a pattern and example to all other spectators how to behave. Why then did they revile you? Because every man hates what stands in his way. They wanted So-and-so to be crowned, you wanted another; they stood in your way and you in theirs. You were found to be stronger than they; they did what they could, they reviled what stood in their way. What would you have then? That you should do what you wish, and they should not even say what they wish? Nay, what wonder they should talk so? Do not farmers revile Zeus, when He stands in their way? Do not sailors revile Him? Do they not revile Caesar without ceasing? What follows? Does not Zeus know? Does not Caesar have reported to him what men say? What does he do then? He knows that if he punishes all who revile him he will have no one left to rule over. What is my con-

---

[3] *Pneuma,* "spirit," here used as equivalent to *psyche,* "soul," or *hegemonikon.* The word is used in two other senses by Epictetus: in II. 23 of the "spirit" which makes vision and other sensations possible, and in III. 13 as one of the four elements (with earth, fire, and water) into which man returns at death.

[1] Epirus, to the northwest of Greece: under the early Empire part of the province of Achaea; but this passage shows that at this time Epirus was under a separate governor, a Procurator of equestrian rank.

clusion? When you enter the theater you ought not to say, "Let me have Sophron[2] crowned," but "Let me keep my will in accord with Nature in this matter, for no one is dearer to me than myself: it is absurd then that I should be injured, that another may be victorious on the stage."

Whom then do I want to win? The victor: and so the victory will always be in accordance with my wish.

"But I wish Sophron to be crowned."

Hold as many contests as you please in your own house and proclaim him there victor in the Nemean, Pythian, Isthmian and Olympic games: but in public do not claim more than your share, nor steal what is public property. If you do, you must put up with being reviled: for when you do as the people do, you put yourself on their level.

CHAPTER 5: Against Those Who Make Illness an Excuse for Leaving the Lecture-Room

"I am ill here," says one, "and want to go away home."

What, were you never ill at home? Do you not consider whether you are doing anything here to improve your will, for if you are doing no good, you might just as well never have come? Go away, and attend to your affairs at home: for if your Governing Principle cannot be brought into accord with Nature, no doubt your bit of land will prosper; you will add to your bit of money! You will tend your old father, frequent the marketplace, serve as a magistrate, do anything that comes next, poor wretch, in your wretched way. But if you understand that you are getting rid of bad judgements and gaining others in their place, and that you have transferred your attention from things outside the will's control to things within it, and that now if you cry, "Ah me!" it is not for your father or your brother but for yourself that you cry, then why should you take account of illness any more? Do you not know that disease and death are bound to overtake us whatever we are doing? They overtake the farmer at his farming, the sailor on the seas. What would you like to be doing when they overtake you? For you must needs be overtaken, whatever you are doing. If you can find anything better than this to be doing when you are overtaken, do it by all means!

For my own part I would wish death to overtake me occupied with nothing but the care of my will, trying to make it calm, unhindered, unconstrained, free. I would fain be found so employed, that I may be able to say to God, "Did I transgress Thy commands? Did I use the

---

[2] An actor.

faculties Thou gavest me to wrong purpose? Did I use my senses or my primary notions in vain? Did I ever accuse Thee? Did I ever find fault with Thy ordinance? I fell sick, when it was Thy will: so did others, but I rebelled not. I became poor when Thou didst will it, but I rejoiced in my poverty. I held no office, because it was Thy will: I never coveted office. Didst Thou ever see me gloomy for that reason? Did I ever come before Thee but with a cheerful face, ready for any commands or orders that Thou mightest give? Now it is Thy will for me to leave the festival. I go, giving all thanks to Thee, that Thou didst deign to let me share Thy festival and see Thy works and understand Thy government." May these be my thoughts, these my studies, writing or reading, when death comes upon me!

"But I am ill, and shall not have my mother to hold my head."

Go to your mother then; for you deserve to be ill, with her to hold your head.

"But I had a nice bed to lie on at home."

Go to your nice bed then; sick or well you deserve to lie on a bed of that sort! Pray do not lose what you can do there.

But what does Socrates say? "As one man," he says, "delights to improve his field, and another his horse, so I delight in following day by day my own improvement."

"In what? In paltry phrases?"

Man, hold your peace.

"In pretty precepts then?"

Enough of that.

"Nay, but philosophers busy themselves with nothing else, so far as I see."

Is it nothing (do you think?) never to accuse any one, God or man, never to blame any, to go in and out with the same countenance? These are the things which Socrates knew, and yet he never said that he knew or taught anything; and if any one asked for phrases or precepts, he would take him away to Protagoras or Hippias.[1] In the same way if any one had come looking for greenstuff, he would have taken him to the gardener. Which of you then makes this[2] the purpose of his life? Why, if you did, you would gladly suffer sickness and hunger and death. If any one of you was ever in love with a pretty girl, he knows that I speak true!

---

[1] Protagoras of Abdera, one of the most distinguished sophists of the fifth century B.C., who lived for many years in Athens; Hippias of Elis, one of the most famous of the sophists, contemporary with Socrates.
[2] That is, the ideal of Socrates, peace of mind.

CHAPTER 6: Scattered Sayings

When one of his acquaintances asked why more progress was made in old days, although the processes of reason have been more studied by the men of today, he answered, On what has the effort been spent, and in what was the greater progress in the past? for you will find that progress today corresponds exactly to the effort spent. The fact is that today men have spent their effort on the analysis of syllogisms, and progress is made in that: in old days men spent their effort on maintaining their mind in accord with Nature, and they made progress in that. Therefore do not confound the processes, nor seek to spend effort on one thing and make progress in another. If you look whether any of us who sets himself to keep in accord with Nature and to live his life so, fails to make progress, you will find there is none.

"The good man can suffer no defeat."

Of course, for he engages in no contest where he is not superior. "Take my lands, if you will: take my servants, take my office, take my poor body, yet you will not make me fail to get what I will or fall into what I will to avoid." This is the only contest for which he enters—that which is concerned with the sphere of the will, and therefore he cannot fail to be invincible.

When some one asked him what "general perception" meant, he replied, You might describe the faculty which only distinguishes sounds as "general" hearing, but the faculty which distinguishes musical sounds you would not call "general" but "technical." In the same way there are certain things which all men who are not utterly perverted can see in virtue of their general faculties. It is this mental constitution to which the name "general perception"[1] is given.

It is not easy to give stimulus to young men who have no grit: "you cannot lift a cream-cheese by a hook": but young men of parts hold fast to reason even if you try to deter them. That is why Rufus generally tried to deter them, and made this his test of those who were gifted and those who were not; "for," said he, "just as the stone, if you throw it up, will fall to the earth by its own nature, so the gifted soul is all the more inclined towards its natural object, the more you try to beat it off."

---

[1] The perception common to man, by which, unless his nature is perverted, he can see certain elementary moral notions.

CHAPTER 7: Dialogue with the Commissioner of the Free Cities, Who Was an Epicurean

When the Commissioner,[1] who was an Epicurean, came into his lecture-room, It is proper, said Epictetus, that we who are ignorant should inquire of you philosophers what is the Best Thing in the world, just as those who come to a strange city make inquiry of the citizens who know the place; that having learnt what it is we may pursue it for ourselves, and come to the sight of it, as foreigners visit the sights of the cities. For all, one may say, are agreed that man has to do with three things, soul and body and external things; it only remains for you to answer the question, "What is the *best* in man?" What shall we say to men? Shall we say, "The flesh"? and was it for this that Maximus sailed as far as Cassiope to see his son on his way?[2] Was it to have pleasure in the flesh? When the Commissioner denied it, saying, "God forbid!" Epictetus went on, Is it not proper to devote our efforts to what is best in us?

"It is most proper."

What have we then better than the flesh?

"The soul," he said.

And which are better, the goods of the best element in us or the goods of the inferior?

"Those of the best."

Are the goods of the soul in the sphere of the will or beyond it?

"Within the sphere of the will."

Is the pleasure of the soul then within the sphere of the will?

"Yes," he said.

And what gives rise to it? Does it arise of itself? That is inconceivable; for we must assume the existence of the good as something which has value in itself, by partaking in which we shall have pleasure in the soul.

To this too he agreed.

What then will give rise to this pleasure of the soul in us? If the goods of the soul give rise to it, then the nature of the good is discovered; for it is impossible that the good and that which gives us rational delight should be different from one another, or that the consequence should be good unless that on which it depends is good. For the primary end must be good, if that which follows on it is to be rational. But you cannot say this if you have any sense, for you will be saying what is incon-

---

[1] Such special commissioners, sent to set in order the affairs of the "free cities," date from Trajan's reign. We do not know who this commissioner was.

[2] Maximus has been identified with L. Appius Maximus Norbanus, who commanded in a Parthian expedition in Trajan's reign and died in the East. May it not refer to Pliny's friend who was "corrector" of the free cities of Achaea? (Cassiope was a port in Epirus.)

sistent with Epicurus, and with the other judgements of your school. You will be reduced to saying that the pleasure of the soul is pleasure in bodily things: these, as it now appears, are of primary value and are identical with the nature of the good.

Therefore Maximus acted foolishly, if he had any motive in sailing but the flesh, that is the highest principle. He acts like a fool too if, as a judge, he refrains from other men's goods when he can take them. If you think fit to do it, the only point for us to look to is that it be done secretly, securely, without any one's knowledge. For even Epicurus himself does not set down stealing as evil, but only detected stealing: and he says "Do not steal," only because "it is impossible to be sure of escaping detection." But I tell you that if it be done cleverly and cautiously, we shall escape detection. Further, we have powerful friends in Rome, both men and women, and the Greeks are feeble folk: no one will have the courage to go to Rome to prosecute. Why do you refrain from your own good? It is foolish and silly. Nay, even if you tell me you refrain, I will not believe you; for just as it is impossible to assent to what appears false and to reject what is true, so it is impossible to hold aloof from what appears good. Now wealth is a good thing, and, so to speak, most productive of pleasure. Why should not one acquire it? Why should we not corrupt our neighbor's wife, if we can do it without detection; and if her husband talks nonsense, why should we not break his neck as well? This, if you wish to be a philosopher of the right sort, to be perfect and consistent with your own judgements. Otherwise you will be no better than we so-called Stoics, for we too say one thing and do another: we say noble words and do shameful deeds! You will be suffering from the opposite perversion, of uttering shameful judgements, and doing noble deeds!

Before God, I ask you, can you imagine a city of Epicureans?

"I shall not marry" (says one).

"Nor shall I" (says another), "for it is wrong to marry."

Yes, and it is wrong to get children, and wrong to be a citizen!

What is to happen then? Where will your citizens come from? Who will educate them? Who will be Governor of the Ephebi? Who will manage the Gymnasia? Yes, and what will be their education? Will it be the education the Lacedaemonians or Athenians received? Take me a young man and bring him up in accordance with your judgements. The judgements are bad, subversive of the city, ruinous to family life, not even fit for women. Man, leave these principles alone. You live in an imperial city: you must hold office, judge justly, refrain from other men's property: no woman but your wife must seem fair in your eyes, no boy, no silver or gold plate. You must look for judgements that will be in keeping with such conduct, and will enable you to refrain with pleasure from things so persuasive to attract and to overcome you. If on the other hand we back up their persuasive power by this philosophy, such as it is, that we have discovered, thrusting us forward and confirming us in the same direction, what is to become of us? What is the best part of a piece of plate, the silver or the art spent on it? The hand in itself is mere flesh, it is the products of the hand that claim precedence. So too appropriate actions are of three kinds:[3] the first class relative to mere existence, the second relative to particular conditions, the third commanding and absolute. On this principle too we ought not to honor man's material being, his rags of flesh, but his leading characteristics. What are these? Citizenship, marriage, procreation of children, worship of God, care of parents, and in general, will to get and to avoid, impulse to act and not to act, each in its proper and natural manner.

What is our nature? To be free, noble, self-respecting. What other animal blushes? What other can have a conception of shame? We must subordinate pleasure to these principles, to minister to them as a servant, to evoke our interests and to keep us in the way of our natural activities.

"But I am rich, and have need of nothing."

Why then do you still pretend to be a philosopher? Gold and silver plate are enough for you: what need have you of judgements?

"Nay, but I also sit as judge over the Greeks."

What! you know how to judge? What made you know that?

"Caesar wrote me a patent."

Let him write to you to judge questions of music: what use will it be to you? But let that pass. How did you get made a judge? Whose hand did you kiss? Was it Symphorus' or Numenius'?[4] In whose antechamber did you sleep? To whom did you send gifts? After all, do you not see that being judge is worth no more nor less than Numenius is worth?

"Well, but I can put any one I wish in prison."

As you may a stone!

"But I can cudgel to death any one I wish."

As you can an ass! This is not governing men. Govern us as rational creatures by showing us what is expedient, and we will follow it: show us what is inexpedient and we will turn away from it. Make us admire and emulate you, as Socrates made men do. He was the true ruler of

---

[3] The classification is obscure and not very relevant here. The division appears to imply a distinction between actions concerned with outward existence (the first and second class) and those concerned with man's higher life (the third class). The former have only a relative, the latter an absolute, value.

[4] Symphorus and Numenius are not known: they were probably freedmen who had risen to high position.

men, for he brought men to submit to him their will to get and to avoid, their impulse to act and not to act.

"Do this, refrain from this, or I will put you in prison." This is not how rational beings are ruled. But, "Do this as Zeus ordained: if not, you will suffer penalty and harm." What kind of harm? No harm but that of failing to do your duty: you will destroy the trustworthy, self-respecting, well-behaved man in you. Look not for any greater harm than this!

CHAPTER 8: How We Should Train Ourselves to Deal with Impressions

As we train ourselves to deal with sophistical questions, so we ought to train ourselves day by day to deal with impressions: for these too propound questions to us.

"The son of So-and-so is dead."
Answer, That is beyond the will, not an evil.
"So-and-so's father has disinherited him: what do you think?"
It is outside the will, not an evil.
"Caesar has condemned him."
That is outside the will, not an evil.
"Something has made him grieve."
That is an act of will, and evil.
"He has endured nobly."
That is an act of will, and good.

If we acquire this habit, we shall make progress, for we shall never assent to anything but that of which we get a convincing impression.[1]

The son dies. What happens?
The son dies.
Nothing more?
Nothing.
The ship is lost. What happens?
The ship is lost.
He is led to prison. What happens?
He is led to prison. Each man may add, "He has fared ill," but if so, that is his own affair.

"Still," you say, "Zeus does wrong to act so."

---

[1] A technical term of the Stoics for an overmastering impression which convinces those to whom it comes of its truth. It is, as Bonhöffer says, not so much the criterion of truth but the symptom by which the subject recognizes the presence of truth. It is not clear whether the adjective means "that lays hold of the mind," or "that gets a grasp on reality."

Why? Do you mean because He made you patient, noble-minded, because He saved these things from being evil, because He puts it in your power to endure these troubles and still be happy, because He "opens the door" to you, when your position is impossible? Leave the scene, man, and do not complain.

If you would know the attitude of the Romans to philosophers, listen to this. Italicus,[2] a man of the highest repute as a philosopher among them, in my presence expressed his indignation at his lot, which he thought intolerable, by saying, "I cannot bear it: you are ruining me, you will make me like him," and pointed to me!

CHAPTER 9: To a Rhetor Going Up to Rome for a Trial

When a man, who was going to Rome for an action regarding his official position, came in to see him, he inquired the reason for his journey, and when the man went on to ask him his opinion on the matter, "If you ask me," he said, "what you will do in Rome, whether you will succeed or fail, I have no precept to offer: but if you ask me how you will do, I can say this, that if your judgements are right you will do well, if wrong, you will do ill. For every man's action is determined by a judgement. What is it that made you desire to be elected patron of the Cnossians?" Judgement.[1]

What is the reason you now go to Rome? Judgement. Yes, and in stormy weather and at your own risk and charges?

"Necessity compels me."

Who tells you this? Your judgement. If then judgements are the cause of everything and a man has bad judgement, the result resembles the cause, whatever this be. Have we all then sound judgements? Have you and your opponent? Then how are you at variance? Have you sound judgements any more than he? Why? You think so. So does he, and so do madmen. Opinion is a bad criterion. No! Show me that you have examined your judgements and paid attention to them. You are now sailing to Rome to be patron of the Cnossians and are not content to stay at home with the honors you had before, but desire some greater and more distinguished honor. When did you ever take the trouble to sail like this in order to examine your judgements and reject any that are bad? Whom have you ever consulted for this purpose? What time

---

[2] Unknown.

[1] Every municipal town in Italy and the provinces had one or more "patrons," who were supposed to represent them in Rome, but the relation was often purely honorary. Cnossus was the chief town of Crete, with a Roman colony.

or what part of your life have you charged with this duty? Review the seasons of your life in your own mind, if you respect me. Did you examine your judgements when you were a boy? Did not you do what you did then as you do everything now? And when you grew to be a youth and listened to the teachers of rhetoric and wrote declamations of your own, what did you imagine that you lacked? And when in early manhood you began to enter public life and to plead in cases and to have a reputation, did you ever think any one your equal? Would you ever have let any one examine you and show that your judgements were bad? What then would you have me tell you?

"Give me some help in the matter."

I have no precepts to offer for your purpose: and if you have come to me for this, you have come to me as you would come to a greengrocer or a shoemaker and not as to a philosopher.[2]

"For what purpose then have philosophers precepts to offer?"

For this: that, whatever the issue may be, we should keep our Governing Principle in accord with Nature to our life's end. Do you think this a small matter?

"No, the greatest of all."

Well then: will a little time suffice for this, and can it be acquired in a passing visit? Acquire it if you can!

Then you will go away and say, "I met Epictetus, it was like meeting a stone, or a statue."

Yes, for you just saw me and no more. Man can only meet man properly when he gets to understand his convictions and shows him his own in turn. Get to know my judgements, and show me yours, and then say that you have met me. Let us question one another: if one of my judgements is bad, remove it: if you have anything to say, put it forward. That is how to meet a philosopher. That's not your way, but "We are passing through: while we wait to charter our ship, we can see Epictetus; let us see what he is saying." Then when you leave you say, "Epictetus was nothing: he talked bad Greek, outlandish stuff." Of course, of what else are you competent to judge, coming in like that?

"But," he goes on, "if I let myself be absorbed in these things, I shall be like you without land, like you without silver cups, like you without fine cattle."

To this perhaps it is sufficient to answer, I have no need of them: but if you get a large property, you still need something else, and willy-nilly you are poorer than I.

"What do you mean that I need?"

---

[2] *I.e.*, you have come to me to buy ready-made judgements, as if they were goods from a tradesman, instead of coming for live inspiration.

You need what you have not got—tranquillity, a mind in accord with Nature, and free from perturbation. Whether I am Patron or not, what does it matter? It does matter to you. I am richer than you: I am not in an agony as to what Caesar will think of me: I do not flatter any one for that. This is what I have instead of your silver and gold plate. You have vessels of gold, but your reason—judgements, assent, impulse, will—is of common clay. But mine are in accord with Nature, and that being so, why should I not make a special study of reasoning? I have leisure, and my mind is not distracted. How can I occupy my mind that is thus free? I cannot find an occupation more worthy of man than that. When you have nothing to do, you are troubled in spirit, and enter a theater, or wander aimlessly. Why should not the philosopher devote his efforts to developing his own reason? You devote yourself to crystal vases, I to the syllogism called "the Liar": you to murrhine[3] vessels, I to the syllogism of "Denial." To you all that you have appears small: to me all I have appears great. Your desire can never be fulfilled, mine is fulfilled already. Your case is like that of children putting their hand into a narrow-necked jar and pulling out raisins and almonds. If a child fills his hand full, he cannot pull it out and then he cries. Let a few go, child, and you will get it out. So I say to you, "Let your desire go." Do not crave much, and you will obtain.

CHAPTER 10: How One Should Bear Illnesses

We should have each judgement ready at the moment when it is needed: judgements on dinner at dinner-time, on the bath at bathing-time, on bed at bedtime.

> *Admit not sleep into your tender eyelids*
> *Till you have reckoned up each deed of the day—*
> *How have I erred, what done or left undone?*
> *So start, and so review your acts, and then*
> *For vile deeds chide yourself, for good be glad.*

Keep hold of these lines for practical use, not to declaim them as a cry like "Paean Apollo." Again in a fever we must be ready with judgements for that; if we fall into a fever we must not give up and forget everything, and say, "If I ever study philosophy again, may the worst befall me! I must go off somewhere and attend to my poor body." Well, but does not fever come there? What does studying philosophy mean?

---

[3] These were vases of valuable material and varied markings, but whether of natural stone or of glass is uncertain.

Does it not mean preparing to face events? Do you not understand then that what you are saying comes to this, "If I go on preparing to bear events quietly, may the worst befall me?" That is as though a man should give up competing for the pancration because he has been struck. But there it is possible to leave off and so escape a beating: but what profit do we get if we leave off studying philosophy?

What ought one to say then as each hardship comes? "I was practising for *this*, I was training for *this*." God says to you, "Give me a proof, whether you have kept the rules of wrestling—eaten the proper food, trained, and obeyed the trainer." After that, are you going to play the coward when the moment of action comes? If now is the time for fever, take your fever in the right way; if for thirst, thirst in the right way, if for hunger, hunger aright. Is it not in your power? Who will hinder you? The physician will hinder you from drinking, but he cannot hinder you from thirsting aright: he will hinder you from eating, but he cannot hinder you from hungering in the right way.

"But am I not a student?"[1]

Why are you a student? Slave, is it not that you may be happy and have peace of mind? Is it not that you may conform to nature and so live your life? What hinders you in a fever from keeping your Governing Principle in accord with nature? Here is the test of the matter, this is how the philosopher is proved. For fever too is a part of life, like walking, sailing, travelling. Do you read when you are walking? No. Nor do you in a fever: but if you walk aright, you have done your part as a walker; if you bear your fever aright, you have done your part as a sick man. What does bearing fever rightly mean? It means not to blame God or man, not to be crushed by what happens, to await death in a right spirit, to do what you are bidden; when the physician comes in, not to be afraid of what he may say, and if he says, "You are doing well," not to be overjoyed: for what good is there in that? What good had you when you were in health? It means not to be disheartened if he says, "You are doing badly"; for what does "doing badly" mean? It means drawing near the dissolution of the soul from the body. What is there to fear in that? If you do not draw near now, shall you not draw near later? Is the world going to be turned upside down by your death? Why then do you coax the physician? Why do you say, "Master, if you will, I shall get well?" Why do you give him occasion to lift his brow in arrogance? As you give the shoemaker his due in regard to the foot, the builder in regard to the house, why do you not give the physician his due (and no more) in regard to the paltry body, for the body is not

---

[1] The objector suggests that as a student of philosophy he is above these petty considerations. Epictetus reminds him of the purpose of philosophy.

mine and is naturally dead? This is what the moment requires from the man in a fever: if he fulfils these requirements, he has what is his own.

It is not the business of the philosopher to guard these outward things—paltry wine or oil or body—but to guard his Governing Principle. How is he to regard outward things? Only so far that he does not concern himself with them unreasonably. What occasion is left then for fear? What occasion for anger, what occasion for fear concerning things that are not our own, nor of any value? For the two principles we must have ready at command are these: that outside the will there is nothing good or evil, and that we must not lead events but follow them. "My brother ought not to have behaved so to me." No, but it is his business to look to that; however he may behave, I will deal with him as I ought. This is my part, that is another's: this no one can hinder, that is subject to hindrance.

CHAPTER 11: Scattered Sayings

There are certain punishments ordained as it were by law for those who disobey the government of God. Whoever judges anything to be good except what depends upon the will, let him be liable to envy, desire, flattery, distraction. Whoever judges anything else to be evil (save acts of the will), let distress be his, and mourning, lamentation, misfortune. And yet, though we suffer punishments so severe, we cannot refrain.

Remember what the poet says about the stranger:

> *Stranger, though baser man than thou should come,*
> *He must be honored, for the hand of Zeus*
> *Guards stranger folk and poor.*

One should be ready to apply this to a father: "Though a baser one than thou should come, I may not dishonor a father; for all depend on Zeus, God of our fathers," and to a brother, "for all depend on Zeus, God of kindred." In the same way we shall find that Zeus is Protector of all other relations of life.

CHAPTER 12: On Training

We ought not to train ourselves in unnatural or extraordinary actions, for in that case we who claim to be philosophers shall be no better than mountebanks. For it is difficult to walk on a tight-rope, and not only difficult but dangerous as well: ought we for that reason to practice walking on a tight-rope or setting up a palm tree, or embracing statues?[1] By no means. Not everything that is difficult and dangerous is suitable for training, but only that which is conducive to what is set before us as the object of our effort. What is set before us as the object of our effort? To move without hindrance in the will to get and the will to avoid. And what does that mean? Not to fail in what we will nor to fall into what we avoid. To this end, therefore, let our training be directed: for since it is impossible without great and continuous effort to secure that the will to get fail not and the will to avoid be not foiled, know that, if you allow training to be directed to things lying outside and beyond the will, you will not get what you will to get nor avoid what you will to avoid.

And since habit has established a strong predominance, because we have acquired the habit of turning our will to get and our will to avoid only to what lies outside our control, we must set a contrary habit to counteract the former, and where impressions are most likely to go wrong there employ training as an antidote.

I am inclined to pleasure: in order to train myself I will incline beyond measure in the opposite direction. I am disposed to avoid trouble: I will harden and train my impressions to this end, that my will to avoid may hold aloof from everything of this kind. For how do we describe the man who trains? He is the man who practices avoiding the use of his will to get, and willing to avoid only what is in the sphere of the will and who exercises himself in what is hard to overcome. And so different men have to train for different objects. What is it to the purpose here to set up a palm tree, or to carry about a hut of skins or a pestle and mortar?[2] Man, train yourself, if you are arrogant, to bear with being reviled, and not to be annoyed when you are disparaged. Then you will make such progress that, even if you are struck, you will say to yourself, "Imagine that you have embraced a statue." Next train yourself to use wine properly, not for heavy drinking—for there are men misguided enough to train for this—but first to abstain from wine, and to leave alone pretty maids and sweet cakes. Then, if the proper time comes, you will enter the lists, if at all, to try yourself and learn whether your impressions overcome you as before. But to begin with, fly far from enemies that are stronger than you. The battle is an unequal one when it is between a pretty maid and a young man beginning philosophy. "Pot and stone," as the saying is, "do not agree."

Next after the will to get and the will to avoid comes the sphere of

---

[1] "Setting up a palm tree" seems to be mentioned as an acrobatic feat. Embracing statues was one of Diogenes' forms of self-discipline in winter.
[2] The tent and the pestle and mortar are the furniture of "the simple life."

impulse for action and against action: where the object is to obey reason, not to do anything at the wrong time or place, or offend the harmony of things in any other way.

Third comes the sphere of assents, concerned with things plausible and attractive. For, as Socrates bade men "not live a life without examination," so you ought not to accept an impression without examination, but say, "Wait, let me see who you are and whence you come," just as the night-watch say, "Show me your token." "Have you the token given by nature, which the impression that is to be accepted must have?"

And to conclude, the methods which are applied to the body by those who exercise it, may themselves conduce to training, if they tend in this direction, that is, if they bear upon the will to get and the will to avoid. But if their object is display, they are the marks of one who has swerved from the right line, whose aims are alien, one who is looking for spectators to say, "What a great man!" This is why Apollonius[3] was right in saying, "If you wish to train for your soul's sake, when you are thirsty in hot weather take a mouthful of cold water and spit it out and tell no one!"

CHAPTER 13: What a "Forlorn" Condition Means, and a "Forlorn" Man

The "forlorn" state is the condition of one without help. For a man is not forlorn simply because he is alone, any more than a man in a crowd is unforlorn. At any rate when we lose a brother or a son or a friend, in whom we rest our trust, we say that we have been left forlorn, though often we are in Rome, with that great throng meeting us in the streets, and those numbers living about us, and sometimes we have a multitude of slaves. For according to its conception the term "forlorn" means that a man is without help, exposed to those who wish to harm him. For this reason, when we are travelling, we call ourselves forlorn most of all, when we fall among robbers. For it is not the sight of a man as such that relieves us from being forlorn, but the sight of one who is faithful and self-respecting and serviceable. For if being alone is enough to make one forlorn, you must say that Zeus Himself is forlorn at the Conflagration of the Universe[1] and bewails Himself: "Unhappy me! I have neither Hera nor Athena nor Apollo nor, in a word, brother or son

---

[3] Pythagorean philosopher of Tyana in Cappadocia.

[1] The universe was believed to be in periodic process, and to be consumed in a conflagration at the end of each period.

Book Three

or grandson or kinsman." And in fact this is what some say that He does, when left alone in the Conflagration: for they cannot conceive of the mode of life of a solitary Being: they start with a natural principle, the fact that men are by nature drawn by ties of fellowship and mutual affection, and enjoy converse with their kind. But nevertheless a man must prepare himself for solitude too — he must be able to suffice for himself, and able to commune with himself. Just as Zeus communes with Himself and is at peace with Himself and reflects upon the nature of His government, and occupies Himself with thoughts appropriate to Himself, so should we be able to talk to ourselves, without need of others, or craving for diversion: we should study the divine government and the relation in which we stand to other things: we should consider what was our attitude to events before, and what it is now: what the things are which still afflict us: how they may be cured, how removed: if any things need to be brought to perfection, perfect them as reason requires.

For see: Caesar[2] seems to provide us with profound peace; there are no wars nor battles any more, no great bands of robbers or pirates: we are able to travel by land at every season, and to sail from sunrise to sunset. Can he then provide us also with peace from fever, from shipwreck, from fire or earthquake or thunderbolt? Go to, can he give us peace from love? He cannot. From mourning? He cannot. From envy? No! he cannot give us peace from any of them. But the reasoning of philosophers promises to give us peace from these troubles also. What does it say? "Men, if you attend to me, wherever you may be, whatever you may be doing, you will feel no distress, no anger, no compulsion, no hindrance, but will live undisturbed and free from all distractions." When a man has this peace proclaimed to him, not by Caesar (how could *he* proclaim it?) but proclaimed by God, through the voice of reason, is he not content when he is alone? When he considers and reflects, "Now no evil can befall me, robber exists not for me, earthquake exists not: all is full of peace and tranquillity: every road, every city, every meeting, neighbor, companion — all are harmless. Another,[3] Who takes care of me, supplies food and raiment; He has given me senses and primary conceptions; and when He does not provide necessaries, He sounds the recall, He opens the door and says, 'Come.'" Where? To nothing you need fear, but to that whence you were born, to your friends and kindred, the elements. So much of you as was fire shall pass into fire, what was earth shall pass into earth, the spirit into spirit, the water into water. There is no Hades, nor Acheron, nor

---
[2] Trajan after his conquest of Dacia.
[3] God.

Cocytus, nor Pyriphlegethon,[4] but all is full of gods and divine beings. When one has this to think upon, and when he beholds the sun and moon and stars, and enjoys land and sea, he is not forlorn any more than he is destitute of help.

"Nay," you say, "but what if one come upon me alone and murder me?"

Fool, he murders not you, but your paltry body.

How can we speak any more than of being forlorn and helpless? Why do we make ourselves worse than children? For what do children do when they are left alone? They pick up potsherds and dust and build something or other and then pull it down and build something else again, and so they never lack diversion. If you sail away, am I to sit and shed tears because I am left alone and forlorn? Shall I not in that case have my potsherds and my dust? But they do this in their foolishness: do we in our wisdom make ourselves miserable?

Great power is always dangerous in a beginner.[5] We must then bear such things according to our strength, but always according to nature. A certain course may suit a strong man but not a consumptive. Be content to practice the life of an invalid, that you may one day live the life of a healthy man. Take scant food, drink water: refrain from willing to get anything for a while, that you may one day direct your will rationally. If you do so, then, when you have some good in you, you will direct your will aright.

"No," you say, "we want at once to live as wise men and benefit mankind."

Benefit indeed! What are you after? Did you ever benefit yourself?

"But I want to stir them up."

Have you stirred yourself up first? You want to benefit them; then show them in your own life what sort of men philosophy makes, and cease to talk folly. When you eat, benefit those who eat with you, when you drink, benefit those who drink, by yielding and giving way to all, by bearing with them: that is the way to benefit them and not by venting your own phlegm[6] upon them!

CHAPTER 14: Scattered Sayings

As bad actors cannot sing alone, but only in a large company, so some men cannot walk alone. Man, if you are worth anything, you must walk

---
[4] The rivers of Hades.
[5] The connection of this section with the preceding sections is obscure. The general sense is that a beginner in philosophy must not behave as though he were a past-master.
[6] Probably refers to "the consumptive." It is the drivel of the sickly novice in philosophy.

alone, and talk to yourself and not hide in the chorus. Learn to bear mockery, look about you, examine yourself, that you may get to know who you are.

When a man drinks water, or puts himself in training in any way, he tells everybody at every opportunity, "I am a water drinker." What? Do you drink water for the sake of drinking it? Man, if it is to your profit to drink it, drink; if not, your conduct is absurd. I say, if you drink water because it does you good, say nothing to those who dislike it. What? Are these the people of all others that you wish to please?

Actions have varying degrees of value: some are based on first principles,[1] others are determined by circumstances, or compromise, or compliance, or manner of life.

There are two qualities that men must get rid of—conceit and diffidence. Conceit is to think that one needs nothing beyond oneself: diffidence is to suppose that one cannot live the untroubled life in the midst of so many difficulties. Now conceit is removed by cross-questioning, and that was what Socrates began with: that the thing is not impossible you must discover by thought and search. This search will do you no harm: and indeed philosophy means very little else but this—to search how it is practicable to exercise the will to get and the will to avoid without hindrance.

"I am better than you, for my father is of consular rank." Another says, "I have been tribune, and you have not." If we were horses you would say, "My sire was swifter," or, "I have plenty of barley and fodder," or, "I have fine trappings." If you said that, you may imagine me replying, "Very well then, let us try our paces." Come, is there nothing in men, like the pace of a horse, which will enable us to distinguish the better from the worse? Are there not self-respect, honor, justice? Show yourself superior in these qualities, that you may be superior as a man should be. If you say to me, "I am great at kicking," I shall answer, "That is the boast of an ass!"

CHAPTER 15: That We Should Approach Everything with Consideration

In everything you do consider what comes first and what follows, and so approach it. Otherwise you will come to it with a good heart at first because you have not reflected on any of the consequences, and afterwards when difficulties come in sight you will shamefully desist.

---

[1] Things or actions of primary importance as opposed to what is opportunist and accidental.

"I wish to win at the Olympic games."

"So do I, by the gods, for it is a fine thing."

Yes, but consider the first steps to it and what follows: and then, if it is to your advantage, lay your hand to the work. You must be under discipline, eat to order, touch no sweets, train under compulsion, at a fixed hour, in heat and cold, drink no cold water, nor wine, except to order; you must hand yourself over completely to your trainer as you would to a physician. Then, when the contest comes, you get hacked,[1] sometimes dislocate your hand, twist your ankle, swallow plenty of sand, get a flogging,[2] and with all this you are sometimes defeated. First consider these things and then enter on the athlete's career, if you still wish to do so: otherwise, look you, you will be behaving like the children, who one day play at athletes, another at gladiators, then sound the trumpet, next dramatize anything they see and admire. You will be just the same—now athlete, now gladiator, then philosopher, then orator, but nothing with all your soul. Like an ape you imitate everything you see, and one thing after another takes your fancy, but nothing that is familiar pleases you, for you undertake nothing with forethought; you do not survey the whole subject and examine it beforehand, but you take it up half-heartedly and at random. In the same way some people when they see a philosopher, and hear some one speaking like Euphrates[3] (and indeed who can speak as he can?) wish to be philosophers themselves.

Man, consider first, what it is you are undertaking: then consider your own powers, and what you can bear. If you want to be a wrestler, look to your shoulders, your thighs, your loins. For different men are born for different things. Do you suppose that you can be a philosopher if you do as you do now? Do you suppose that you can eat and drink as you do now, and indulge your anger and displeasure just as before? Nay, you must sit up late, you must work hard, conquer some of your desires, abandon your own people, be looked down on by a mere slave, be ridiculed by those who meet you, get the worst of it in everything—in office, in honor, in justice. When you have carefully considered these drawbacks, then come to us, if you think fit: if you are willing to pay this price for peace of mind, freedom, tranquility. If not, do not come near: do not be like the children, first a philosopher, then a tax-collector, then an orator, then one of Caesar's procurators. These callings do not agree. You must be one man, good or bad: you must develop either your rational soul, or your outward endowments, you must

---

[1] The precise meaning is uncertain, possibly "get hacked" (*cf.* our colloquial use of the word "dig" in "a dig in the ribs") or "get covered with dust."

[2] Flogging would be a punishment for fouling or any other breach of the rules.

[3] An eloquent Stoic contemporary of Epictetus.

be busy either with your inner man, or with things outside, that is, you must choose between the position of a philosopher and that of an ordinary man.

When Galba was killed some one said to Rufus, "Now the world is governed by Providence, isn't it?" To which he answered, "Did I base my proof that the world is governed by Providence upon a casual thing like Galba's death?"[4]

CHAPTER 16: **That We Must Be Cautious in Our Social Relations**

The man who mixes with other people a good deal either for talk or for a wine-party or generally for social purposes, must needs either grow like them himself or convert them to his likeness; for if you put a quenched coal by one that is burning, either it will put the burning one out, or will catch fire from it. As the risk then is so serious, you must be cautious in indulging lightly in the society of the untrained, for it is impossible to rub up against one who is covered with soot and not get sooty oneself. What are you going to do, if he talks about gladiators, about horses, about athletes, worse still if he talks about men: "So and so is bad," "So and so is good": "That was well done," "That was ill done": again, if he mocks or jeers, or shows a malicious humour? Has any of you the perfect skill of the lyre-player, who takes up his lyre and has only to touch the strings to know which are out of tune and so tune his instrument? Which of you has the faculty that Socrates had, of drawing to his side those who met him in any kind of society? How could you have? *You* must needs be converted by your untrained companions.

Why then are they stronger than you? It is because these unsound sayings of theirs are based upon judgements, but your fine words come merely from your lips: that is why they are without life or vigor, that is why a man may well loathe the sound of your exhortations and your wretched "virtue," which you prate of so glibly. That is how the untrained get the better of you: for judgement is powerful everywhere, judgement suffers no defeat. Therefore, until your fine ideas are firmly fastened in you, and until you acquire some power to secure them, I advise you to be cautious in associating with the untrained: otherwise anything you take note of in the lecture-room will melt away day by day like wax in the sun. Therefore go away somewhere far from the sun, as long as your ideas are in this waxen state. For this reason philosophers

---

[4] *I.e.*, such a conclusion demands serious, systematic study. (Galba was emperor for six months after Nero's fall [A.D. 68–9].)

even advise us to leave our own countries, because old habits are a drag on us and prevent us from beginning to acquire a new set of habits, and we cannot bear men meeting us and saying, "Look, So-and-so is turning philosopher, behaving like this and like that." On the same principle physicians send away patients who are ill for long to a new country and a new climate, and rightly so. Do the same. Adopt new habits: fix your opinions, exercise yourselves in them. No, you leave the lecture-room to go to a show, a gladiatorial display, a colonnade, a circus: then you come back here from them and return there again, and nothing affects you. So you acquire no habit that gives you distinction; you pay no regard or attention to yourself: you do not watch yourself and ask, "How do I deal with the impressions that meet me? Naturally, or unnaturally? How am I to answer their call? Rightly or wrongly? Do I warn things beyond my will that they have no concern with me?" I say, if you are not yet in this state, then fly from your former habits, fly from the uneducated, if you wish to begin at last to be more than ciphers.

CHAPTER 17: Concerning Providence

When you accuse Providence, only consider the matter, and you will understand that its action is according to reason.

"But the unjust man," you say, "is better off."

In what? In money: for in regard to this he has the advantage over you, because he flatters, is shameless, is vigilant. Is this surprising? But look whether he is better off than you in being trustworthy and self-respecting. You will find that he is not; where you are superior to him, you will find that you are better off. So when some one was indignant once at the prosperity of Philostorgos,[1] I said, "Would you be willing to share the bed of Suras?"[2] "May that day never come!" he said. "Why then are you indignant at his getting a return for what he sells, or how do you come to count him blessed who gets what he has by means that you abhor? Or what is the harm in Providence giving the better lot to those who are better? Is it not better to be self-respecting than to be rich?"

He agreed.

Man, why are you indignant then at having the better lot? Therefore always remember the truth and be ready to apply it—that it is a law of nature for the better to have the advantage of the worse in that in which he is better, and then you will never be indignant.

---

[1] A rich but degraded man.
[2] Possibly Palfurius Sura, an orator said to have been expelled from the Senate by Vespasian; afterwards an informer under Domitian; he was condemned on Domitian's death.

"But my wife uses me ill."

Very well: if any one asks you, "What is the matter?" say, "My wife uses me ill."

"Nothing else?"

Nothing.

"My father gives me nothing" . . . but need you go further in your own mind and add this lie, that poverty is evil? For this reason it is not poverty that we must cast out, but our judgement about poverty, and so we shall be at peace.

CHAPTER 18: That We Must Not Allow News to Disturb Us

When any disturbing news is brought you, bear this in mind, that news cannot affect anything within the region of the will. Can any one bring news to you that you are wrong in your thought or wrong in your will? Surely not: but only that some one is dead; what does that concern you? That some one speaks ill of you; what does that concern you? That your father has some design or other. Against whom? Is it against your will? How can he have? No, it is against your wretched body, or your wretched property; you are safe, it is not against *you*.

But the judge pronounces that you are guilty of impiety. Did not the judges pronounce the same on Socrates? Is it your concern that the judge pronounced on you? No. Why then do you trouble yourself? Your father has a duty of his own, which he must fulfil, or else lose his character as father, affectionate and gentle. Do not try to make him lose anything else for that reason; for a man never suffers harm except in that in which he is at fault.

Again, it is your duty to make your defense with firmness, self-respect, dispassionately: otherwise you lose your character as son, self-respecting and honorable. What then? Is the judge free from danger? No: he too incurs danger just as much. Why then do you still fear what judgement he will give? What have you to do with another's evil? Your evil is to defend yourself badly: that is the only thing you need be careful about. Whether you are condemned or not condemned is another's business, and the evil in the same way is another's.

"So-and-so threatens you."

Threatens me? No.

"He blames you."

It will be for him to see how he does his own business.

"He is going to condemn you unjustly."

All the worse for him!

CHAPTER 19: What Is the Difference Between the Philosopher and the Uneducated Man

The first difference between the philosopher and the uneducated man[1] is that the latter says, "Woe is me for my child, for my brother, woe is me for my father," and the other, if he is compelled to speak, considers the matter and says, "Woe is me for myself." For nothing outside the will can hinder or harm the will; it can only harm itself. If when we accept this, and, when things go amiss, are inclined to blame ourselves, remembering that judgement alone can disturb our peace and constancy, I swear to you by all the gods that we have made progress.

Instead of this we have come the wrong way from the beginning. When we were still children, if we stumbled when we were stargazing, the nurse, instead of rebuking us, struck the stone. What is wrong with the stone? Was it to move out of the way because of your child's folly? Again, if (when children) we do not find something to eat after our bath our attendant does not check our appetite, but flogs the cook. Man, did we appoint you to attend on the cook? No, on our child: correct him, do him good. So even when we are grown up we appear like children: for it is being a child to be unmusical in musical things, ungrammatical in grammar, uneducated in life.

CHAPTER 20: That Benefit May Be Derived from All Outward Things

In regard to intellectual impressions it is generally agreed that good and evil depend upon us and not upon external things. No one calls the proposition, "It is day," good, or "It is night," bad, or "Three is four," the greatest of evils. No, they say that knowledge is good and error evil, so that good may arise even in regard to what is false; that is, the knowledge that it is false. The same ought to be true in practical life.

"Is health good, and disease evil?"

No, man.

"What then?"

To use health well is good, to use it ill is evil.

"Do you mean that benefit can be gained even from disease?"

---

[1] *Idiotes* is the layman, who has had no philosophic training and is therefore unskilled in the art of living.

By heaven, can it not be gained even from death, aye or from lameness?[1] Do you think Menoeceus gained but little good by his death?[2]

"Nay, if any one says that sort of thing, I wish him a benefit like that Menoeceus gained!"[3]

Out upon you, man, did he not preserve the patriot, the man of great mind, trustworthy and noble? And if he had lived on, was he not bound to lose all these, and win their very opposite? Would he not in that case have assumed the character of the coward, the ignoble, the hater of his country and lover of his life? Go to, do you think he gained but little good by his death? Well, did Admetus' father[4] gain great good by living on so ignobly and miserably? Did he not die afterwards? I adjure you by the gods, cease to admire material things, cease to make yourselves slaves, first of things, and next, for their sake, of men who can acquire them or take them away.

"Can we then get benefit from these things?"

From all.

"Even from one who reviles us?"

Why, what good does the athlete get from the man who wrestles with him? The greatest. So my reviler helps to train me for the contest: he trains me to be patient, dispassionate, gentle. You deny it? You admit that the man who grips my neck and gets my loins and shoulders into order does me good, and the trainer does well to bid me "lift the pestle with both hands," and the more severe he is, the more good do I get: and are you going to tell me that he who trains me to be free from anger does me no good? That means that you do not know how to get any good from humankind.

"He is a bad neighbor," you say?

Yes, for himself: but he is good for me; he trains me to be considerate and fair-minded.

"A bad father."

Yes, for himself, but not for me. This is the magic wand of Hermes. "Touch what you will," he says, "and it will turn to gold." Nay, bring what you will and I will turn it to good. Bring illness, bring death, bring poverty, bring reviling, bring the utmost peril of the law-court: the wand of Hermes will turn them all to good purpose!

"What will you make of death?"

---

[1] Perhaps a reference to Epictetus himself.
[2] Menoeceus, son of Creon, according to Greek legend sacrificed himself to save Thebes.
[3] The sarcastic answer of an opponent.
[4] Admetus' father, a typical instance of desire for long life, familiar from the *Alcestis* of Euripides.

What else but an adornment for you, what else but a means for you to show in deed what man is when he follows the will of nature?

"What will you make of sickness?"

I will show its nature, I will shine in it. I will be firm and tranquil, I will not flatter my physician nor pray for death. What more do you look for? Whatever you give me I will make it a means of blessedness and happiness, make it dignified and admirable.

That is not your way. You say, "See you do not fall ill, it is an evil." It is like saying, "See you do not get an impression that three is four, it is an evil." Man, how is it an evil? If I get a right notion of it, it cannot harm me any more. Will it not rather do me good? If then I have proper notions of poverty, of sickness, of life without office, is not that enough for me? Will they not serve my good? How then should I seek any more for good and evil in things external?

But we do not act on this. We carry these views to the lecture-room door, but no one takes them home: as soon as we leave here we are at war with our slave-boy, with our neighbors, with those who jeer and laugh at us. Good luck to the Lesbian, for he convicts me every day of knowing nothing.[5]

CHAPTER 21: To Those Who Undertake the Profession of Teacher with a Light Heart

Those who have learnt precepts and nothing more are anxious to give them out at once, just as men with weak stomachs vomit food. First digest your precepts, and then you will not vomit them: undigested, they become vomit indeed, impure and uneatable. Show us that you have digested them to some purpose, and that your Governing Principle is changed, as athletes can show their shoulders, as a result of their training and eating, and as those who have acquired the arts can show the result of their learning. The carpenter does not come and say, "Hear me discourse on carpentry," but he undertakes a contract and builds a house and so shows that he has acquired the art. Do you likewise: eat as a man, drink as a man, adorn yourself, marry, get children, live a citizen's life; endure revilings, bear with an inconsiderate brother, bear with a father, a son, a travelling companion. Show us that you can do this, and then we shall see that you have in truth learnt something from the philosophers. Not you: you say, "Come and hear me reading out

---

[5] The connection is not quite clear. "The Lesbian," as Upton suggests, may be a slave or a scoffer; Epictetus, by way of reproof to those who quarrel with the first person they meet, wishes good luck to his slave for reminding him of his ignorance.

comments!" Away with you, look for some one to disgorge your vomit on.

"I assure you I will expound Chrysippus' doctrines to you as no one else can. I will break up his language and make it quite clear. I will add, it may be, a touch of Antipater's or Archedemus' verve."

What! is it for this that young men are to leave their countries and their parents, that they may come and hear you expounding petty points of language? Ought they not to return ready to bear with others and work with them, tranquil and free from tumult, furnished with a provision for life's journey, which will enable them to bear what befalls them well and to adorn themselves thereby? And how are you to impart to them what you do not possess yourself? For your sole occupation from the first has been this—how you are to resolve syllogisms and variable arguments, and arguments concluding with a question.

"But So-and-so gives lectures, why should not I?"

Slave, you cannot do this off-hand, and in a random fashion. It demands mature years, and a certain way of life, and the guidance of God.

You say no: but no one sails from harbor without sacrificing to the gods and invoking their help, and men do not sow at random, but only when they have invoked Demeter; and when a man has laid his hand to a task so momentous as this without the gods' help, will he be secure and will those who come to him be fortunate in their coming? Man, what are you doing but making the Mysteries common? You say, "There is a shrine at Eleusis,[1] lo, here is one also: there is a hierophant there: I too will make a hierophant: there is a herald there, I too will appoint a herald: there is a torch-bearer there, I too will have a torch-bearer: there are torches there, so there are here: the cries are the same. What difference is there between our doings and the Mysteries?"

Most impious of men, is there no difference? The benefit of the Mysteries depends on proper place and time: one must approach with sacrifice and prayer, with body purified and mind ready and disposed to approach holy rites and ancient sanctities. Only so do the Mysteries bring benefit, only so do we arrive at the belief that all these things were established by those of old for our education and the amendment of our life. But you publish and divulge them out of place and out of season, without sacrifices or purifying: you have not the dress which the hierophant should have, nor the proper hair, nor the fillet: you have not the right voice nor age, you have not lived pure as he has, but you have merely learnt off the words and say, "The words have a holy power in themselves."

---

[1] Northwest of Athens, the home of the great Mysteries of Demeter and Persephone.

You must approach the task in another fashion: it is momentous and full of mystery, not a chance gift which any one can command. The care of the young demands, it may be, more than wisdom: yes, by Zeus, one must have a certain readiness and special fitness, and a certain habit of body, and above all the counsel of God advising one to discharge this duty, as He counselled Socrates to examine men, and Diogenes to rebuke men in royal fashion, and Zeno[2] to instruct and lay down precepts. You open a doctor's consulting-room with nothing but some drugs, without ever taking the trouble to acquire a knowledge of when or how they are applied. "See, that's his remedy, eye-salve" (you say): "I have that too." Have you also the faculty of using it? Do you know when and how and to whom it will do good? Why then do you play at hazard with matters of highest moment, why are you reckless, why do you take in hand a task unsuited to your powers? Leave it to those who can do it and do it with distinction.

Do not bring disgrace upon philosophy by your personal act, nor join those who disparage the profession; but if the study of precepts really attracts you, sit quietly and turn them over in your mind, but never call yourself a philosopher nor allow any one else to do so, but say: "He is in error: I am unchanged; my will, my impulses, my assent, are what they were, and, in a word, I have not advanced from my position, but deal with impressions as before." So think, so speak about yourself, if you would think aright. But if this is beyond you, then play at hazard and do as you are doing, for you will be acting in character.

CHAPTER 22: On the Calling of the Cynic

When one of his acquaintance, who seemed inclined to the Cynic School, asked him what should be the character of the Cynic,[1] and what was the primary conception of the school, he said, We will consider it at leisure: but this much I can tell you, that he who undertakes so great an enterprise without God's help is under God's wrath, and has no other wish but to disgrace himself in the public eye, for in a well-managed house a man does not come forward and say to himself, "I ought to be steward": for, if he does, the master of the house takes notice, and when he sees him swaggering and ordering people about, he drags him away and gives him the lash. So it happens also in this great

---

[2] The founder of Stoicism.

[1] Nowhere else does Epictetus so completely adopt the Cynic name as in this chapter. The Cynic whom he describes is the ideal Stoic teacher, who is distinguished from the ordinary Stoic by a more austere and isolated life.

City of the Universe. Here, too, there is a Master of the House who assigns each thing its place.

"You are the sun: your faculty is to revolve and make the year and the seasons, to give growth and increase to the fruits, to rouse the winds and bring them to rest and to give temperate warmth to men's bodies; go, travel on your course and so move all things from the greatest to the least."

"You are a calf: when a lion appears, do your part, or you will suffer for it." "You are a bull, come near and fight: for this is your proper portion and lies within your powers." "You can lead the army against Ilion: be Agamemnon." "You can fight Hector in single combat: be Achilles." But if Thersites[2] came forward and claimed the command he would not get it, or if he got it he would be shamed before a multitude of witnesses.

You, like the rest, must give the matter careful thought: it is not what you think. "I wear a coarse cloak now and shall do so then, I sleep hard now and shall still do so, I shall take to myself a wallet and a staff and begin to go about begging and reviling those I meet, and if I see any one using pitch-plasters,[3] or with his hair finely dressed, or walking in scarlet, I shall rebuke him."

If that is your impression of the Cynic's calling, give it a wide berth: do not come near it, for you have no concern with it; but if you have a true impression of it and still deem yourself not unworthy, then consider what a great enterprise you are taking in hand.

First, you must show a complete change in your conduct, and must cease to accuse God or man: you must utterly put away the will to get, and must will to avoid only what lies within the sphere of your will: you must harbor no anger, wrath, envy, pity: a fair maid, a fair name, favorites, or sweet cakes, must mean nothing to you. For you must know that other men, when they indulge in such things, have the protection of their walls and houses and darkness. There are many things to hide them: one, may be, has closed the door, or has set some one to guard his chamber: "If any one comes, say, 'He is out' or 'He is busy.'" But the Cynic, instead of all these, should have self-respect for his shelter: if he has not that, he will be naked and exposed and put to shame. This is his house, his door, this his chamber-guards, this his darkness: for he must not wish to conceal anything that is his: if he does, he disappears; he loses the true Cynic, the free open-air spirit, he has begun to fear outward things, he has begun to have need of concealment, and when he would hide himself he cannot; for he has no place or means to hide

---

[2] The type of ugliness and insolence in the *Iliad*.
[3] To get a smooth skin.

himself. But if by chance the public teacher, the "pedagogue" is caught erring what must be his feelings! Is it possible with these fears before one to be confident with one's whole mind, and command other men? It is impracticable, impossible.

First then you must make your Governing Principle pure, and hold fast this rule of life, "Henceforth my mind is the material I have to work on, as the carpenter has his timber and the shoemaker his leather: my business is to deal with my impressions aright. My wretched body is nothing to me, its parts are nothing to me. Death? Let it come when it will, whether to my whole body or to a part of it. Exile? Can one be sent into exile beyond the Universe? One cannot. Wherever I go, there is the sun, there is the moon, there are the stars, dreams, auguries, conversation with the gods."

The true Cynic when he has ordered himself thus cannot be satisfied with this: he must know that he is sent as a messenger from God to men concerning things good and evil, to show them that they have gone astray and are seeking the true nature of good and evil where it is not to be found, and take no thought where it really is: he must realize, in the words of Diogenes when brought before Philip after the battle of Chaeronea, that he is sent "to reconnoiter."[4] For indeed the Cynic has to discover what things are friendly to men and what are hostile: and when he has accurately made his observations he must return and report the truth, not driven by fear to point out enemies where there are none, nor in any other way disturbed or confounded by his impressions.

He must then be able, if chance so offer, to come forward on the tragic stage, and with a loud voice utter the words of Socrates: "Oh race of men, whither are ye hurrying? What are you doing, miserable creatures? You wander up and down like blind folk: you have left the true path and go away on a vain errand, you seek peace and happiness elsewhere, where it is not to be found, and believe not when another shows the way." Why do you seek it outside? Do you seek it in the body? It is not there. If you doubt, look at Myron, look at Ophellius.[5] In property? It is not there. If you disbelieve, look at Croesus,[6] look at the rich men of today, and see how full their life is of lamentation. In office? It is not there. If it were, then those who have twice or thrice been consuls should be happy, but they are not. Whom shall we trust on this matter?

---

[4] The philosopher is sent into the world to spy out the land, and discover what forces in the world are good and what are evil. (Chaeronea was the site of a great battle in Boeotia in which the combined Athenian and Theban forces were defeated by Philip of Macedon in 338 B.C.

[5] Myron and Ophellius were gladiators.

[6] King of Lydia—the typical rich man.

Shall we trust you who look upon their fortune from outside and are dazzled by the outward show, or the men themselves? What do they say? Listen to them, when they lament and sigh, and think their condition to be more miserable and perilous just because of their consulships and glory and distinction. Shall you find in it royalty? It is not there. If it were, Nero would have been happy, and Sardanapalus.[7] Why, even Agamemnon was not happy, though he was a finer fellow than Sardanapalus and Nero. When the rest were snoring what did he do? *"Many hairs he plucked by the roots from his head,"* and what did he say himself? *"Thus do I wander and am in agony of spirit, and my heart leaps from my breast."*

Miserable man, what is wrong with your affairs? Is it your property? No. Your body? No. You have *"store of gold and copper."* What is wrong with you then? You have neglected and ruined that in you—whatever it be—wherewith we exercise the will to get and to avoid, the impulse to act and not to act. How have you neglected it? It is ignorant of the true nature of the good to which it is born and of the nature of evil, and of what concerns it and what does not. And so when something that does not concern it is in bad case, it says, "Woe is me, the Hellenes are in peril!" Oh miserable mind of man, alone neglected and uncared for!

"They are going to perish, slain by the Trojans!"

And if the Trojans slay them not, will they not die?

"Yes, but not all at once."

What does it matter then? If death is evil, it is equally evil, whether men die alone or together. Will anything else happen, but that body and soul will be separated?

Nothing.

And if the Hellenes perish, is *the door closed* to you? Is not death within your power?

"It is."

Why do you mourn then? Bravo! a king indeed, and holding the scepter of Zeus![8]

A king cannot be miserable any more than God can be. What are you then? A shepherd in very truth, for you weep just like shepherds when a wolf carries off one of their sheep: yes and these whom you rule are sheep too. And why did you come here? Was there any danger to your will to get or your will to avoid, your impulse for action and against action?

"No," he says, "but my brother's poor wife was carried off."

It is a great gain to be robbed of an adulterous wife.

---

[7] King of Nineveh, a typical tyrant.
[8] To a Stoic a "miserable king" is a contradiction, for the wise man is the only king.

"Are we then to suffer the scorn of the Trojans?"

What are they? Are they wise or foolish? If they are wise, why do you make war on them? If they are foolish, what does it matter to you?

In what then does the good reside, since it is not in these things? Tell us, Sir Messenger and Spy.

It is where you think not, and will not seek for it. For if you had wished you would have found it in yourselves and would not have wandered outside and would not have sought the things of others as your own. Turn again to *yourselves*, learn to understand the primary notions which you have. Of what nature do you imagine the good to be?

"Tranquil, fraught with happiness, unhindered."

Nay, but do you not imagine it as naturally great? Do you not imagine it as precious? Do you not imagine it as free from harm? I ask you then, in what subject must we seek for that which is tranquil and unhindered? In the slavish or the free?

"In the free."

Your poor body then, is it slavish or free?

"We know not."

Do you not know that it is a slave to fever, gout, ophthalmia, dysentery, the tyrant, fire, sword, everything stronger than itself?

"Yes, it is a slave."

How then can any part of the body be still free from hindrance? How can that which is naturally dead—earth and clay—be great or precious? What then? Have you no element of freedom?

"Perhaps none."

Why, who can compel you to assent to what appears false?

"No one."

And who to refuse assent to what appears true?

"No one."

Here then you see that there is something in you which is naturally free. What man among you can have will to get or to avoid, impulse to act or not to act, or can prepare or put an object before himself, without conceiving an impression of what is profitable or fitting?

"No one."

Here too then you have free and unhindered action. Miserable men, develop this, set your minds on this, seek your good *here*.

"Nay, but how is it possible for a man who has nothing, naked, without home or hearth, in squalor, without a slave, without a city, to live a tranquil life?"

Lo, God has sent you one who shall show indeed that it is possible. "Look at me, I have no house or city, property or slave: I sleep on the ground, I have no wife or children, no miserable palace, but only earth and sky and one poor cloak. Yet what do I lack? Am I not quit of pain and fear, am I not free? When has any of you ever seen me failing to get what I will to get, or falling into what I will to avoid? When did I blame God or man, when did I accuse any? Has any of you seen me with a gloomy face? How do I meet those of whom you stand in fear and awe? Do I not meet them as slaves? Who that sees me but thinks that he sees his king and master?" There you have the true Cynic's words; this is his character, and scheme of life. No, you say, what makes the Cynic is a little wallet, and a staff and a big pair of jaws; to devour or hoard everything you give him or to revile out of season those who meet him, or to make a show of his fine shoulder!

Is this the spirit in which you mean to take in hand so great an enterprise? Take a mirror first, look at your shoulders, take note of your loins and your thighs. Man, it is an Olympic contest you are about to enter your name for, not a miserable, make-believe match. At Olympia you cannot simply be beaten and leave the grounds; in the first place you must be disgraced in the sight of all the world, not before men of Athens only or of Lacedaemon or of Nicopolis; in the next place the man who lightly enters the lists must be flogged, but before he is flogged he must suffer thirst and scorching heat and swallow plenty of dust. Think it over more carefully, know yourself, inquire of heaven, attempt not the task without God. If He advise you, know that He wishes you to become great or to receive many stripes. For this too is a very fine strand woven into the Cynic's lot: he must suffer strokes like an ass and love the very men that strike him as though he were the father or brother of all.

No, no; if a man flogs you, you must stand in the midst and cry aloud, "Caesar, what pains I suffer under your rule of peace! Let us go to the proconsul."

What has the Cynic to do with Caesar or proconsul or any one else but Zeus, Who has sent him upon earth, and Whom he serves? Does he call upon any one but Him? Is he not convinced that whatever pains he suffers are God's training of him? Why, Heracles, when he was being trained by Eurystheus,[9] did not count himself wretched, but fulfilled all his commands without shrinking, and shall this man, who is under the training and discipline of Zeus, cry aloud in indignation, if he be worthy to carry the staff of Diogenes? Listen to what Diogenes said when the fever was on him to those who passed by: "Base creatures," he said, "will you not stay? You go all that way to Olympia to see athletes killed or matched in battle, and yet have you no wish to see a battle between fever and a man?" I suppose you think a man like that would have been very likely to accuse God, Who sent him, of using

---

[9] Legendary king of Tiryns, in whose service Heracles accomplished his labors.

him hardly? Nay, he was proud of his distresses, and was fain to be the spectacle of passers-by. On what ground is he to accuse God? That he is living a seemly life, and that he is displaying his virtue in a clearer light? But what does he say of poverty, of death, of pain? How did he compare his own happiness with that of the Great King? Nay, he did not so much as think it comparable. For where there are tumults, and distresses, and fears, where the will to get is unfulfilled, and the will to avoid is foiled, a world of envies and jealousies, how can happiness find a way there? But wherever there are unsound judgements, there all these passions must be.

And when the young man asked Epictetus, whether, if he fell sick and a friend asked him to come to his house to be tended in his sickness, he was to consent, he said, Where will you find me a Cynic's friend? For he must be another like himself, that he may be worthy to be counted as his friend; he must share with him the scepter and the kingdom and be a worthy minister, if he is to be deemed worthy of his friendship, as Diogenes was worthy of Antisthenes, and Crates of Diogenes.[10] Or do you think that if he salutes him as he comes near that makes him his friend, and the Cynic will count him worthy to receive him in his house? Wherefore, if this is your opinion and such your thoughts, look round rather for a fine dunghill to have your fever on, one that shelters you from the north wind, to save you from a chill. But you seem to me to want to get away into some one's house for a time and eat your fill. How comes it then that you should take in hand so great a matter?

"Will the Cynic," said his questioner, "accept marriage and children as matters of prime importance?"

If, he replied, you grant me a city of wise men, it may be that no one will lightly adopt the Cynic's calling. For what reason should he take upon him this manner of life? But if we assume that he does, there will be nothing to prevent him from marrying and getting children; for his wife will be like himself, and his wife's father will be like him, and his children will be brought up on these lines. But in the present constitution of the world—which is that of the battlefield—it is a question whether the Cynic should not be undistracted entirely, devoted to the service of God, able to go to and fro among men, not tied down to acts that befit private occasions, nor involved in personal relations, which if he violates he will cease to keep his character as a good man, and if he maintains them he will destroy the Messenger and Spy and Herald of the gods that is in him. For he must show services to his father-in-law,

---

[10] Antisthenes, founder of the Cynic School (about 426–356 B.C.); Crates, a Theban pupil of Diogenes the Cynic (*flor.* 320 B.C.).

and render them to his wife's other relations and to herself; and so he is reduced to being a sick nurse or a general provider. Not to speak of other things, he must needs have a saucepan, to make water hot for the baby, to wash him in the bath; when his wife has had a child he must provide wool and oil for her, and a bed and a cup—the vessels mount up at once—not to mention other business and distraction. What becomes now of that king of ours who watches every interest of the public,

Trusted with clans and full of many cares,

whose duty it is to watch others, those who have married and got children, to see which of them uses his wife well, which ill, who is quarrelsome, which house is prospering and which is not, going about like a physician and feeling men's pulses? "You have a fever, you a headache, you the gout; I prescribe fasting for you, food for you, no bath for you; you need the surgeon's knife, you the cautery." How can the man who is involved in the acts appropriate to private life find leisure? Must he not procure clothes for the children? Must he not send them to the schoolmaster with their tablets and note-books, and provide them with beds, for they cannot be Cynics from their mother's womb? If he does not provide for them, it were better to fling them aside as soon as born rather than kill them thus. See to what a pass we bring our Cynic, how we take away his kingdom!—"Yes, but Crates married."

The case you mention was a special one and a love match, and you have to assume a wife who was a Crates herself. Our inquiry is concerned with ordinary marriages which are liable to distraction; and from this point of view we do not find that in these circumstances marriage has a primary claim on the Cynic.

"How then," says he, "will he keep society going?"

By God, do you think that those who bring into the world two or three ugly little squeakers to fill their place do men greater benefit than those who exercise oversight, so far as they can, over all men, to see what they do, how they live, what they attend to, what they undutifully neglect? Do you think the Thebans reaped greater benefit from those who left them children than from Epaminondas[11] who died childless? Did Priam who begat fifty sons, rascals all, or Danaus or Aeolus contribute more to society than Homer? What? Shall a man abstain from marrying or getting children for the sake of acting as general or writing

---

[11] The great general and statesman, who raised Thebes to be the leading power in Greece (379–366 B.C.).

a treatise, and be thought to have got a fair exchange for his childlessness, and shall the kingdom of the Cynic be thought no compensation?

Perhaps we do not realize his greatness nor picture at its true worth the character of Diogenes: we only look at the Cynics of today,

> *Dogs of the table, guardians of the gate,*

who copy those of old in nothing, except perhaps in dirty habits.

If we knew what a Cynic was we should not be moved or astonished at his not marrying or getting children. Man, he is parent to all men, he has men for his sons, women for his daughters; he approaches all and treats all in the spirit of a father. Do you think he reviles those he meets because he is a busybody? He does it as a father, as a brother, and as servant of Zeus, the Father of all.

Nay, ask me if you think well, whether he will take part in politics.

Fool, do you look for a higher form of politics than those he handles now? Is he to come forward and address an Athenian assembly on revenues or ways and means, when he ought to be discoursing to all mankind, alike to Athenians, to Corinthians, and to Romans, not about ways and means or revenues or peace and war, but about happiness and unhappiness, good fortune and bad fortune, slavery and freedom. When a man is engaged in politics of such moment, do you ask me if he is to be a politician? Nay, ask me if he is to hold office. Fool, what office is greater than this that he holds?

Yet such an one has need also of a body of a certain quality; for if he come forward with a consumptive figure, thin and pale, his testimony no longer carries the same force. For he must not only display mental qualities to convince the lay mind that it is possible to be good and noble without the things that they set store by, but his body must show that the plain and simple life of the open air does no harm to the body—"Look you, how my body and I bear witness to this." As indeed Diogenes did; for he went about with the glow of health on his face, and attracted the masses by his bodily presence. But a Cynic who excites pity is like a beggar; every one turns from him and takes offence at him; for he ought not to appear dirty, lest he should scare men away thereby; nay his very squalor should be cleanly and attractive.

Further, the Cynic ought to have great natural grace and quickness of wit (without this he is a driveller, nothing more) that he may be able to give a ready and apposite answer to each question that arises: as Diogenes answered him who said, "Are you the Diogenes who disbelieves in the gods?" by saying, "How can I be when I think the gods hate you?" or again, when Alexander stood over him as he slept and said:

> *Sleep all night long becomes not men of counsel,*

replied, still in his sleep,

Trusted with clans and full of many cares.

But above all, his Governing Principle must be purer than the sun; otherwise he must needs be a gambler and a reckless person; he will be rebuking others when he is involved in evil himself. See what this means. The kings and tyrants of this world have their armed bodyguard which enables them to rebuke certain persons and to punish those who do wrong even though they are wicked themselves, but the Cynic's conscience takes the place of arms and bodyguard and furnishes him with this authority.[12] When he sees that he has watched and toiled for men, and that his sleep has been pure, and that when sleep leaves him he is purer still, and that all the thoughts of his heart have been those of one who is a friend and servant of the gods, and who shares the rule of Zeus, and that everywhere he is ready to say:

Lead me, O Zeus, and lead me, Destiny,

and "If thus the gods would have it, be it so"—then, I ask, why should he not have confidence to speak freely to his brothers, to his children, and in a word to his kinsfolk?

Therefore the man whose mind is thus disposed is not fussy nor impertinent, for when he is inspecting the affairs of men, he is concerned with what is not another's but his own, unless you are to call the general too a busybody, when he inspects and reviews and keeps watch over his soldiers, and punishes those who offend against discipline. But if you rebuke others when you are carrying a nice cake hid under your arm, I shall say to you, "Would not you rather go off into a corner and eat what you have stolen?" What have you to do with other men's concerns? Who are you? Are you the bull or the queen bee? Show me the tokens of your royalty, like those which nature gives her. But if you are only a drone claiming the kingdom of the bees, do not you think that your fellow citizens will make an end of you, as the bees do to the drones?

The Cynic must have the spirit of patience in such measure as to seem to the multitude as unfeeling as a stone. Reviling or blows or insults are nothing to him; he has given his bit of a body to any one who will, to treat it as he pleases. For he remembers that the inferior must needs be conquered by the superior, where it is inferior, and the body

---

[12] See Abbott, *The Son of Man:* "The Cynic is a natural king; he goes about like a Hercules destroying noxious beasts, and like Aesculapius healing diseases—Warrior and Physician in one. In both these capacities he receives from God authority over men, and men recognize it in him, because they perceive him to be their benefactor and deliverer."

is inferior to the multitude, the weaker inferior to them that are stronger. He therefore never enters upon this contest, where he may be conquered, but at once resigns what does not belong to him and does not claim power over slaves. But when it comes to the will and the power of dealing with impressions then you will see what eyes he has, so that you will say, "Argus[13] was blind in comparison." Is there reckless assent, is there vain impulse, will to get which fails, will to avoid which is foiled, purpose incomplete, blame, disparagement or envy? It is on these he concentrates his attention and energy; for the rest he snores and takes his ease, and all is peace. No one robs him of his will or masters that.

Do they master his bit of a body?
Yes.
And his bit of property?
Yes.
And offices and honors?
What does he care for these? When any one tries to frighten him with these fears he says to him, "Get away, look for children to frighten. They think masks fearsome, but I know that they are made of pot, and have nothing inside."

So momentous is the profession you are thinking of. Before God I beg you to wait if you will, and look first to your equipment; for mark what Hector says to Andromache: "Go rather to the house," he says, "and weave":

> War shall be men's concern,
> All men's, and mine in chief.

So truly did he realize his own endowment and her incapacity.

CHAPTER 23: To Those Who Read and Discourse for Display

First say to yourself, what manner of man you want to be; when you have settled this, act upon it in all you do; for in pretty nearly all pursuits we see that done. Athletes first decide what they want to be, and then they act accordingly. If a man is to be a long-distance runner, he takes the diet, the walking, the rubbing, and the gymnastic suited to that; if he is going in for the short course, he alters all this to suit his aim, if for the pentathlon he alters his training still more. You will find the same done in the arts. If you are a carpenter you will have this kind of work; if a smith, you will have that kind. For in everything we do, if

---

[13] The legendary hundred-eyed guardian of Io.

we have no standard to go by, we shall do it ineffectively; if we use the wrong standard, we shall fail completely.

Now we have two standards to go by, one general and one special. The first is that we must act as human beings. What does this include? We must not act like a sheep, at random, nor like a brute, destructively. The special standard is relative to each man's occupation and purpose. The lyre-player must act as a lyre-player, the carpenter as a carpenter, the philosopher as a philosopher, the orator as an orator. When therefore you say, "Come and hear me lecturing to you," see to it first that you are not acting without aim. Then if you find you have a standard, see to it that it is the right one.

Do you wish to do men good or to receive compliments?

At once you have the answer, "What account do I take of the praise of the multitude?"

An excellent answer. Nor does the musician heed the multitude, so far as he is a true musician, nor the geometrician. Do you wish then to do good? What are you aiming at? Tell us, that we too may run to your lecture-room. Now can any one do good to others unless he has received good himself? No, no more than the man who is no carpenter can help others in carpentry, or he who is no shoemaker in shoe-making.

Would you really know then whether you have received any good? Produce your judgements, my philosopher. What does the will to get profess? Success in getting. And the will to avoid? Escape from what it avoids. Well, do we fulfil their profession? Tell me the truth, and if you lie, I will tell you myself. When lately your audience were slack in their attendance, and did not applaud you, you went away in low spirits. Again when you were lately praised you went round and said to every one, "What did you think of me?"

"I thought you wonderful, master, as I live."

"How did I give that passage?"

"Which do you mean?"

"Where I described Pan and the Nymphs."

"Superlatively."

And yet you tell me that in respect to that will to get and will to avoid you behave in a natural way. Go to, get some one else to believe you! Did you not lately praise So-and-so against your real opinion? Did you not flatter So-and-so, the senator's son? Did you want your children to be like that?

"Heaven forbid!"

Why then did you praise him and pay him attention?

"He is a young man of parts, and ready to listen to arguments."

How do you know that?

"He admires me."

Now you have stated the true reason. After all, what do you think? Do not these very admirers secretly despise you? When a man who is conscious of no good action or good thought meets a philosopher who says, "Here is a genius, frank and unspoilt," do not you think he is bound to say to himself, "This man wants something from me"? Tell me, what sign of genius has he displayed? Why, he has been with you all this long time, he has heard you discoursing, he has heard you lecturing. Has he grown modest? Has he returned to himself?[1] Has he realized what misery he is in? Has he cast away his vanity? Is he looking for some one to teach him?

"He is."

Some one to teach him how he should live? No, you fool, but how he should speak, for that is what he admires you for. Listen and hear what he says: "This man is a perfect artist in style, his style is much finer than Dio's."[2] That's a different thing altogether. Does he say, "This man has self-respect, he is trustworthy and tranquil-minded"? If he did say so, I should say, "Since he is trustworthy, tell me what you mean by this 'trustworthy' man," and if he could not answer I should add, "First learn what your words mean, and then speak."

If you are in this sorry state, gaping for men to praise you, and counting your audience, do you really want to do others good?

"Today I had a much larger audience."

"Yes, it was a large one."

"I suppose five hundred."

"Nonsense! put them at a thousand."

"Dio never had so large an audience."

"How is that?"

"Why, they have a fine turn for understanding arguments."

"Noble teaching, master, can move even a stone."

There you have the words of a philosopher![3] These are the feelings of one who is to benefit mankind, there you have a man who has listened to reason, who has read the teaching of Socrates in the spirit of Socrates, and not as so much Lysias or Isocrates![4] "'I have often wondered by what arguments'—no, 'by what argument'—the singu-

---

[1] The notion is partly of a man "returning to himself," partly of turning his attention to his true self.
[2] Dion Chrysostom of Prusa in Bithynia, a contemporary of Epictetus; his orations are good specimens of the discourses of the Greek teachers or "sophists" of that day.
[3] The words are ironical.
[4] Lysias, an Attic orator of the fourth century B.C., famous for the charm of his plain style; Isocrates, one of the ten Greek orators, a contemporary of Demosthenes, and master of a fluent and finished style.

lar is smoother than the plural."[5] Did you ever read the words except as one reads paltry songs? If you had read them properly you would not have dwelt on these points of language, but would rather have studied the passage, "Anytus and Meletus[6] can kill me, but they cannot harm me," and this, "My nature is such that I cannot attend to my affairs, but only to the argument which appears best to me when I reflect." That was why no one ever heard Socrates say, "I know and teach"; no, he sent one man here, another there; and therefore they used to come to him, asking to be introduced by him to philosophers, and he took and introduced them. No, of course, as he went with them he would say, "Come and hear me discourse today in the house of Quadratus!"[7]

What am I to hear from you? Do you want to display to me your fine composition? Man, you compose well enough, and what good does it do you?

"Do praise me, I beg."

What do you mean by praise?

"Say 'Bravo!' to me, or 'Marvellous!'"

Very well, I say it; but if praise is what philosophers put in the category of the good, what praise can I give you? If correct speaking is a good thing, teach me that, and I will praise you.

"What? are you bound to dislike listening to fine oratory?"

Heaven forbid! I do not dislike listening to a harp-player, but am I therefore bound to stand and play the harp? Hear what Socrates says, "It would not be seemly for me, sir, at this time of life, to come before you like a youth framing fine phrases." "Like a youth," he says. Yes, it is indeed a pretty art, to select fine phrases and put them together, and then come forward and read them or recite them with ability, and as one reads to add, "There are not many that can understand what I say, as sure as you hope to live."

Does the philosopher invite men to a lecture? Does he not draw to him those who are going to get good from him, as the sun draws sustenance to itself? No physician worth the name invites men to come and be healed by him, though I hear that in Rome today physicians do invite them; in my day physicians were called in by their patients.

"I bid you to come and hear that you are in a bad way, that you

---

[5] The words "I have often . . . arguments" are from the beginning of Xenophon's *Memorabilia*. The point is that the discourses of Socrates are treated as matters of language and style, without regard for their substance.
[6] Two of the accusers of Socrates in the trial which ended in his condemnation and death 399 B.C.
[7] Rich Romans lent their houses for lectures and recitations. (C. Ummidius Quadratus was governor of Lusitania in A.D. 37 and of Syria *c*. A.D. 50–60.)

attend to everything rather than what you should attend to, and that you do not know what is good and what is evil, and are unhappy and miserable."

A fine invitation!

Surely, unless the philosopher's words force home this lesson, they are dead and so is he. Rufus was wont to say, "If you find leisure to praise me, my words are spoken in vain." Wherefore he spoke in such fashion that each of us as he sat there thought he was himself accused: such was his grip of men's doings, so vividly did he set each man's ills before his eyes. The philosopher's school, sirs, is a physician's consulting-room. You must leave it in pain, not in pleasure; for you come to it in disorder, one with a shoulder put out, another with an ulcer, another with fistula, another with headache. And then you would have me sit there and utter fine little thoughts and phrases, that you may leave me with praise on your lips, and carrying away, one his shoulder, one his head, one his ulcer, one his fistula, exactly in the state he brought them to me. Is it for this you say that young men are to go abroad and leave their parents and friends and kinsmen and property, that they may say, "Ye gods!" to you when you deliver your phrases? Was this what Socrates did, or Zeno, or Cleanthes?

You ask, "Is there not the hortatory style?"

Yes—no one denies it—just as there is the style for proof and the style for teaching. Who has ever named a fourth style along with them, the ostentatious? What is the hortatory style? The power of showing to one and to many what a sordid struggle they are plunged in, and how they pay regard to everything rather than to what they want. For they want what tends to happiness, but they seek it in the wrong place. Is it for this that you must set up a thousand benches[8] and invite men to come and hear you, and then mount the rostrum in a fine robe or an elegant cloak and describe the death of Achilles? Cease, by all your gods, to dishonor noble words and subjects, so far as in you lies. Nothing is more effective in exhortation than when the speaker makes plain to his hearers that he has need of them.[9] Tell me, in all your readings or discourses, did you ever make one of your audience anxious about himself or rouse him to a sense of his position? Did you ever send one away saying, "The philosopher has got a good grip of me: I must act so no more?" Why, even if your fame is at its height, he only says to some one, "A pretty description that about Xerxes!" while another puts

---

[8] *I.e.*, a big gallery or theater.

[9] *I.e.*, that there is a spiritual relation between them. As God has need of the world (to exhibit his reason), so the true teacher has something to give, which his hearers cannot do without, just as he cannot do without them.

in, "No, the battle of Thermopylae."[10] Is this what a philosopher's lecture comes to?

CHAPTER 24: That We Ought Not to Spend Our Feelings on Things Beyond Our Power

If a thing goes against another's nature, you must not take it as evil for you; for you are born not to share humiliation or evil fortune, but to share good fortune. And if a man is unfortunate, remember that his misfortune is his own fault; for God created all men for happiness and peace of mind. To this end He gave men resources, giving each man some things for his own, and some not for his own, things subject to hindrance and deprivation and compulsion not for his own, but things beyond hindrance for his own. The true nature of good and evil He gave man for his own, as was natural for Him to do, Who cares for us and protests us as a Father.

"Oh, but I have just parted from such an one, and he is distressed!"

Why did he count as his own what was not his? When he rejoiced to look on you why did he not reflect that you are mortal, and that you may go on a journey? Wherefore he pays the penalty for his own foolishness. But why do you bewail yourself, and to what end? Did not you study this distinction either? Did you, as worthless women do, regard all the things in which you took pleasure—places, persons, ways of life—as though they would always be with you? And so now you sit and weep because you do not see the same persons and pass your time in the same place. No doubt you deserve this fate—to be more wretched than rooks and ravens, who may fly where they will and change their nests, and cross the seas, without lamenting or longing for their first possessions.

"Yes, but this happens to them because they have no reason."

Is our reason then given us by the gods for misfortune and misery, that we may continue in wretchedness and mourning? Or would you have all men to be immortal, and no one go abroad? Are we never to go away but all to stay rooted like plants, and if one of our close friends goes abroad are we to sit and weep: and again, if he return, are we to dance and clap like little children?

Shall we not at last give up the milk of babes, and remember what we heard from the philosophers, unless we took what they said for enchanters' tales? "This world is one city, and the substance of which it is

---

[10] The pass between Thessaly and Locris, defended against Xerxes by Leonidas and three hundred Lacedaemonians in 480 B.C.

constructed is one; and things must needs move in a cycle, one thing giving way to another, and some things must pass away, and others come into being, some must abide as they are and others must move; and the universe is full of friends—the gods first, and after them men, whom nature has made akin to one another; some of them must be with one another and others must go away, and we should rejoice in those that are with us, yet not be sad at those who go away. And man, besides being born to a high courage, and to despise all that is beyond his will, has this too for his own, that he is not rooted nor attached to the earth, but goes now to one place, now to another, at one time under the pressure of business, at another merely to see the world." Such indeed was the lot of Odysseus:

> *Cities of many men he saw, and learnt*
> *Their mind;*

and yet earlier it was the lot of Heracles to go about all the inhabited world,

> *Beholding laws and insolence of men,*

cleansing the world and casting forth the insolent, and bringing in the rule of law. Yet how many friends, think you, had he in Thebes, how many in Argos, how many in Athens, and how many did he win for himself as he went about, seeing that he married a wife, where he thought fit, and got children, and forsook his children, with no mourning nor longing, nor as one leaving them orphans? For he knew that no man is an orphan, but that all men have always the Father Who cares for them continually; for to him it was no mere tale that he had heard that Zeus is the Father of men, for he believed Him to be his own father and called Him so, and all that he did he did as looking to Him, wherefore it was in his power to live happily everywhere. But happiness and longing for what is absent can never be united; for that which is happy must needs have all that it will, and be as it were in a state of satisfaction; no thirst or hunger must come near it. But Odysseus, you say, had a sense of longing for his wife, and sat upon a rock and wept. Do you take Homer for your authority in everything, and Homer's stories? If Odysseus really wept, was he not miserable, and what good man is ever miserable? The universe is indeed managed ill if Zeus does not take care of His citizens, that they may be happy as He is. It is not lawful or right even to think of such a thing, and if Odysseus wept and lamented, he was no good man. For how can a man be good, when he knows not who he is, and how can he know this when he has forgotten that all things that have come into being are perishable, and that it is impossible for man to be with man for ever? Now to desire what is impossible is slavish and silly; it is to make oneself a stranger in the world, and to fight against God with one's own judgements, as alone one can.

"But my mother mourns because she does not see me."

Why does she not take to heart these lessons? Yet I do not say that we must not take pains to prevent her lamenting; but that we must not wish absolutely for what is not ours. Another's sorrow is no concern of mine, my sorrow is my own; and so I shall absolutely check my own sorrow, for it is in my power, but another's I shall try to check only so far as I can, but not absolutely; otherwise I shall fight against God, I shall set myself against Zeus and array myself against His conduct of the universe, and the penalty for this battling with God and this disobedience will be paid not only by "children's children," but by me in my own person, by day and by night, when I start in my dreams and am disturbed, when I tremble at every message, when my peace of mind hangs upon another's letters.

Some one is come from Rome.

"If only it be no ill news!"

What ill can happen to you in a place where you are not?

From Greece.

"If only it be no ill news!"

On this principle, every place can cause you misery. Is it not enough that you should be miserable where you are yourself? Must you needs be miserable overseas, and by letter? Is this what you mean by being secure?

What happens then if your friends there die?

What else except that mortal men have died? How can you wish at the same time to grow old and not to see the death of any that you love? Do you not know that in the long course of time many events of divers sorts must happen? One man must be overcome by fever, another by a robber, a third by a despot. For such is the nature of the atmosphere about us, and of our companions; cold and heat and unsuitable food, and travel by land, and sea, and winds and manifold perils destroy one man and send another into exile, and another they send on an embassy or as a soldier. Sit still then with your wits dazed at all these things—mourning, unfortunate, miserable, depending on something other than yourself—not one thing or two, but things innumerable.

Is this what your lesson comes to, is this what you learnt in the philosopher's school? Do you not know that life is a soldier's service? One man must keep guard, another go out to reconnoitre, another take the field. It is not possible for all to stay where they are, nor is it better so. But you neglect to fulfil the orders of the general and complain, when some severe order is laid upon you; you do not understand to what a pitiful state you are bringing the army so far as in you lies; you do not see that if all follow your example there will be no one to dig a trench, or raise a palisade, no one to keep night watch or fight in the field, but every one will seem an unserviceable soldier.

Again, if you go as a sailor on shipboard, keep to one place and hold fast to that; if you are called on to climb the mast, refuse, if to run out on the bows, refuse that. Why, what ship's master will put up with you, and not fling you overboard like a useless bit of furniture, a mere hindrance and bad example to the other sailors? So too it is in the world; each man's life is a campaign, and a long and varied one. It is for you to play the soldier's part—do everything at the General's bidding, divining His wishes, if it be possible. For there is no comparison between that General and the ordinary one in power and superiority of character. You are set in an imperial City and not in some humble town; you are always a senator. Do you not know that such an one can attend but little to his own household? He must spend most of his time abroad, in command or under command, or as subordinate to some officer, or as soldier or judge? And yet you tell me you want to be attached like a plant and rooted in the same place?

"Yes, for it is pleasant."

Who denies it? Dainties are pleasant too, and a beautiful woman is a pleasant thing. Your talk is the talk of those who make pleasure their end.

Do you not realize whose language you are using, the language of Epicureans and abandoned creatures? and yet though your actions and your principles are theirs, you quote to us the words of Zeno and Socrates? Fling away from you, as far as may be, these alien properties that you adorn yourself with, and that do not fit you! People of that sort have no wish except to sleep without hindrance or compulsion, and then to get up and yawn at their ease and wash their face, then to write and read at their pleasure, then to talk nonsense and be complimented by their friends, whatever they say, then to go out for a walk and after a little walk to have a bath, then to eat, and then go to sleep—the sort of sleep men of that kind are likely to indulge in—I need say no more—you may judge what it is.

Come, now, tell me the way of life your heart is set on—you who profess to admire truth and Socrates and Diogenes. What do you want to do in Athens? Just what you are doing? Nothing else? Then why do you call yourself a Stoic? If those who speak falsely of the Roman constitution are seriously punished, are those who speak falsely of so great and serious a subject and a name to get off scot free? That cannot be; none may escape this divine and mighty law, which exacts the greatest punishments from those whose offence is greatest. What does it say? "He that pretends to qualities that concern him not, let him be given to vanity and arrogance; let him that disobeys the divine government be an abject slave, let him be subject to pain, envy, pity, in a word, let him be miserable and full of lamentations."

"What is your conclusion? Would you have me court this great man or that and frequent his doorstep?"

If reason so determine, for country's sake or kindred or mankind, why should you not go to him? You are not ashamed to go to the shoemaker when you want shoes, nor to the market-gardener when you want lettuces. Are you ashamed to go to the rich when you want something they can give?

"Yes, but I do not admire the shoemaker."

Do not admire the rich man either.

"I shall not flatter the market-gardener."

Do not flatter the rich man either.

"How then am I to get what I want?"

Do I say to you, "Go, and you will get what you want," or only, "Go, and act up to your character"?

"Why do I go then?"

That you may come away feeling that you have fulfilled the acts required of a citizen, a brother, a friend. But remember that you have gone to a shoemaker, a greengrocer, one who has no authority over great or high matters, though he sell what he has for a big price. You are going as it were to fetch lettuces; they are worth an obol, but not a talent.

Apply this principle. The business is worth going to a man's door for. Very well, I will go. It is worth an interview. Very well, I will have an interview with him. But if I must kiss his hand and flatter him with compliments, that is like paying a talent. I will have none of it. It is not to my profit, nor to the profit of the city or my friends to ruin a good citizen and a friend.

"But men will think you took no pains if you fail."

Have you again forgotten why you went there? Do you not know that a good man does nothing for the sake of what men think, but only for the sake of doing right?

"What does he gain by doing right?"

What does a man gain who writes Dio's name correctly? The gain of writing.

"Is there no further reward?"

Do you look for any greater reward for a good man than to do what is noble and right? At Olympia you do not want anything else; you are content to have been crowned at Olympia. Does it seem to you so small and worthless a thing to be noble and good and happy? Therefore, since the gods have made you a citizen of this city and you are bound to set your hand betimes to a man's work, why hanker after nurses and the breast, and allow silly women to soften you and make you effeminate with their tears? Will you then never cease to be a babe? Do you not know that he who acts like a child is ridiculous in proportion to his years?

Did you not see any one in Athens, or go to any one's house?

"Yes, the man I wanted to see."

Do the same here; choose to see the man you want, and you will see him; only do it in no abject spirit, without will to get or to avoid, and all will be well with you; but it does not depend on going or standing at the door, but on the judgements that are within you. When you have come to despise things without you and beyond your will's control, and have come to regard none of them as your own, but only this—to be right in judgement, in thought, in impulse, in will to get and to avoid, what room is left for flattery or abjectness of mind? Why do you still long for the peace of your home, and for your familiar haunts? Wait a little and these places[1] will become familiar to you in their turn. Then if your spirit is as degenerate as this, go weep and mourn as soon as you are again parted from these.

"How then am I to prove myself affectionate?"

In a noble and not a miserable spirit. For it is against all reason to be of an abject and broken spirit and to depend on another and to blame God or man. Prove yourself affectionate, but see that you observe these rules; if this affection of yours, or whatever you call it, is going to make you a miserable slave, it is not for your good to be affectionate. Nay, what prevents you loving a man as one who is mortal and bound to leave you? Did not Socrates love his children? Yes, but as one who is free and bears in mind that the love of the gods stands first, and therefore he failed in none of the duties of a good man, either in his defense, or in assessing his penalty, or earlier still as a member of the council or a soldier in the field. But we abound in every kind of excuse for a mean spirit; with some of us it is a child, with others our mother or our brothers. We ought not to let any one make us miserable, but let every one make us happy, and God above all, Who created us for this. Go to, did Diogenes love no one, he who was so gentle and kind-hearted that he cheerfully took upon him all those troubles and distresses of body for the general good of men? But how did he love? As the servant of Zeus should love, caring for his friends, but submitting himself to God. That was why he alone made the whole world his country, and no special land, and when he was made prisoner he did not long for Athens or for his friends and companions there, but made himself at home with the

---

[1] The places where you now are.

Book Three

pirates who took him and tried to make them better, and afterwards when he was sold he lived in Corinth just as he lived before in Athens; yes, and if he had gone away to the Perrhaebians[2] it would have been just the same. That is how freedom is achieved. That is why he said, "Since Antisthenes freed me, I have ceased to be a slave." How did he free him? Hear what he says: "He taught me what is mine and what is not mine; property is not mine; kinsfolk, relations, friends, reputation, familiar places, converse with men—none of these is my own."

What is yours then?

"Power to deal with impressions. He showed me that I possess this beyond all hindrance and compulsion; no one can hamper me, no one can compel me to deal with them otherwise than I will. Who then has authority over me any more? Has Philip, or Alexander, or Perdiccas, or the Great King? How can they? for he who is to be mastered by men, must first—long before—allow himself to be mastered by things. When a man is not overcome by pleasure, or pain, or reputation, or wealth, and, when it seems good to him, can spit his whole body in the tyrant's face,[3] and so leave this world, whose slave can you call him any more? To whom is he subject? But if he had sought his pleasure by living in Athens, and had allowed life in Athens to have the mastery over him, he would have been in every man's control, and any one who was stronger than he would have had power to cause him pain. You can imagine how he would have flattered the pirates to sell him to an Athenian, that he might one day see the beautiful Peiraeus and the Long Walls and the Acropolis.

Slave, who are you that want to see them? If you are servile and abject what good will they do you?

"Nay, I shall be free."

Show me how you are free. Suppose some one, no matter who, takes you away from your familiar course of life; he has laid hands on you and says, "You are my slave, for it is in my power to prevent you from living as you will, it rests with me to relax your servitude, or to humiliate you; when I choose you can put on a glad face again and go off in high spirits to Athens." What do you say to this man who leads you captive? Whom do you produce to set you free from him?[4] Or do you refuse to look him in the face, and cutting arguments short implore him to let you go? Man, you ought to go to prison rejoicing, hastening

---

[2] A powerful tribe of northern Greece: to go among them means to go into wild outlandish regions.

[3] Probably refers to the story that Nicocreon ordered Anaxarchus' tongue to be cut out, whereupon he bit it off himself and spat it in Nicocreon's face.

[4] *Karpistes*, the man by the touch of whose wand the slave became free, if his master made no counter-claim. The word is used again in IV. 1 and 7.

thither before your gaoler can lay hands on you. What! You decline to live in Rome, and long for Hellas? I suppose you will weep in our faces again, when you have to die, because you are not going to see Athens and have a walk in the Lyceum?

Is this what you went abroad for? Is this why you sought converse with a teacher who might do you good? Good forsooth! Was your object to analyse syllogisms more readily or track out hypothetical propositions? Was it for this reason that you left brother, country, friends, relations, that you might learn this lesson and return? It was not then to secure constancy or peace of mind that you went abroad; it was not that you might be set beyond harm's reach and never blame or accuse any one any more, it was not that no one should be able to injure you, and that so you might maintain your life unhindered in all its relations.

A fine traffic this that you have achieved by your travels—syllogisms and shifting terms and hypothetical arguments! Yes, you had better sit in the market if you think fit, and post up a notice like the druggists. Nay! will you not rather deny knowledge of what you learnt, that you may not get your precepts condemned as useless? What harm has philosophy done you, how has Chrysippus wronged you, that you should prove his labors to be useless by your own act? Not content with the ills you had at home, which were enough to cause you pain and sorrow, even if you had not gone abroad, did you acquire new ills besides?

Yes, and if again you have other friends and companions, and if you attach yourself to another country you will only multiply your causes for lamentation. Why then do you live, only to involve yourself in trouble after trouble and make yourself miserable? What, man! You call this "affection"? Affection indeed! If affection is good, it can cause no evil. If it is evil, I have no concern with it. I am born for what is good for me, not for what is evil.

What then is the proper training for this? In the first place, the principal and most important thing, on the very threshold so to speak, is that when you are attached to a thing, not a thing which cannot be taken away but anything like a ewer, or a crystal cup, you should bear in mind what it is, that you may not be disturbed when it is broken. So should it be with persons; if you kiss your child, or brother, or friend, never allow your imagination to range at large, nor allow your exultation to go as far as it will, but pluck it back, keep it in check like those who stand behind generals driving in triumph and remind them that they are men. In like manner you must remind yourself that you love a mortal, and that nothing that you love is your very own; it is given you for the moment, not for ever nor inseparably, but like a fig or a bunch of grapes at the appointed season of the year, and if you long for it in winter you are a fool. So too if you long for your son or your friend, when it is not given you to have him, know that you are longing for a fig in winter time. For as winter is to the fig, so is the whole pressure of the universe to that which it destroys. And therefore in the very moment that you take pleasure in a thing, set before your mind the opposite impressions. What harm is there in whispering to yourself as you kiss your child, "Tomorrow you will die," and to your friend in like manner, "Tomorrow you or I shall go away, and we shall see one another no more"?

"But such words are of ill omen."

Yes, and so are some incantations, but because they do good, I do not mind, if only they do good. But do you give the name "ill-omened" to anything but what signifies evil? Cowardice is an ill-omened thing, and so is a mean spirit, mourning, sorrow, shamelessness; these are ill-omened words, yet even these we must not hesitate to utter, that we may guard against the things themselves. Do you call any word ill-omened that signifies a process of nature? Say that harvesting ears of corn is ill-omened, for it means destruction of the ears; yes, but not the destruction of the world. Say that the fall of the leaf is ill-omened and the change of the fresh fig into the dry and of grapes into raisins; for all these are changes from a previous state into a new one. This is not destruction but an ordered dispensation and government of things. Going abroad is a slight change; death is a greater change—from what now is, not to what is not, but to what is not now.

"Shall I then be no more?"

You will not be, but something else will be, of which the world now has need; for indeed you came into being, not when you willed it, but when the world had need. For this reason the good man, remembering who he is and whence he has come, and by whom he was created, sets his mind on this alone, how he shall fill his place in an orderly fashion with due obedience to God. To God he says, "Dost Thou want me still to live? I will live as one who is free and noble, in accordance with Thy will; for Thou didst give me freedom from hindrance in what was mine. Hast Thou no more need of me? Then may it be well with Thee; I stayed here until now for Thee and for none other, and so now I obey Thee and depart."

"How do you depart?"

Again, as Thou willest, as a free man, as Thy servant, as one who has learnt what Thou dost command and forbid. But as long as I continue among Thy creatures, whom wouldst Thou have me be? A magistrate or a private person, a senator or a commoner, a soldier or a general, a teacher or the head of a household? Whatever place or post Thou dost commit to my charge, "I will die ten thousand times," to use Socrates' words, "sooner than abandon it." Where wouldst Thou have me be? In

Rome or Athens or Thebes or Gyara?[5] Only remember me there. If Thou dost send me to a place where men cannot live as their nature requires, I shall go away,[6] not in disobedience but believing that Thou dost sound the note for my retreat. I do not abandon Thee: heaven forbid! but I recognize that Thou hast no need of me. But if it be given me to live in accordance with nature, I shall not seek another place than where I am or other society than that in which I am.

Let these thoughts be at your command by night and day: write them, read them, talk of them, to yourself and to your neighbor. Go first to one and then to another, asking him, "Can you help me towards this?" Then if some so-called "undesirable" event befall you, the first immediate relief to you will be, that it was not unexpected. For in all matters it is a great thing to say, "I knew that I had begotten a mortal."[7] For this is what you will say, and again, "I knew that I was mortal. I knew that I might have to go away, that I might be cast into exile, I knew that I might be thrown into prison." Then if you reflect within yourself and ask from what quarter the event has come, you will at once remember, "It comes from the region of things outside my will, which are not mine; how then does it concern me?" Then comes the most commanding question of all: "Who has sent it me?"

The Prince or the General, the City or the Law of the City.

Give it me then, for I must always obey the law in everything.

And further, when your imagination (which is not in your control) bites deep into your soul, struggle against it with your reason, fight it down, suffer it not to grow strong nor to advance the next step, calling up at pleasure what pictures it will. If you are in Gyara do not imagine your way of life in Rome, and the great delights you enjoyed when you lived there and that you would enjoy on your return. No, make your one effort there, to live a brave life in Gyara, as one who lives in Gyara should; and if you are in Rome do not imagine life in Athens, but make life in Rome your one study.

Further, you should put this delight first in place of all others, the delight that comes from understanding that you are obeying God, that not in word but in deed you are fulfilling the part of the good man. What a fine thing it is to be able to say to myself, "I am now putting into action what other men talk big of in the lecture-room, and win a name for paradox. As they sit there it is my virtues they are expounding, it is about me they are inquiring, it is my praise they are singing. I say, Zeus wished to make my experience prove this truth to me, and He wished

---

[5] One of the smaller Cyclades, used as a place of banishment under the Empire.
[6] *I.e.*, "take my life."
[7] A saying attributed to Solon, Anaxagoras, and Xenophon.

to discover for Himself, whether He had a soldier in the true sense, a citizen in the true sense, and to put me forward as a witness to the rest of mankind of what does and does not depend on man's will. "Behold" [He says] "your fears are idle and your desires vain. Do not seek good things outside you but within, or you will not find them." It is on these terms that now He brings me here, and again sends me thither; He shows me to men poor, without office, sick, sends me to Gyara, puts me in prison; not that He hates me—heaven forbid! who hates his best servant?—nor that He takes no thought of me, for He takes thought of the lowliest, but because He is training me and using me as a witness to other men. When I am appointed to such a service as this, it is not for me to consider where or in whose company I am or what they say of me, but rather to spend all my effort on God and His commands and ordinances."

If you always have these thoughts at hand, and make yourself familiar with them and keep them at command, you will never want for one to comfort and strengthen you. For dishonor consists not in having nothing to eat, but in not having reason sufficient to secure you from fear and pain. But if you once win yourself freedom from fear and pain, then tyrants and their guards, and the Emperor's household, will cease to exist for you; you, who have received this high office from Zeus, will not feel the sting of an imperial appointment or of those who offer sacrifice on the Capitol in virtue of their offices.

Only make no display of your office, and boast not yourself in it, but prove it by your conduct; be content, even if no one observes you, to live in true health and happiness.

CHAPTER 25: To Those Who Fail to Achieve What They Set Before Them

Consider which of the aims that you set before you at the first you have achieved, and which you have not, and how some things give you pleasure to remember and some give you pain; and if possible, recover what you failed to obtain. For those who are entering on the greatest of all struggles must not shrink, but must be ready to endure stripes; for the struggle they are concerned with is not wrestling or the pancration, in which a man may succeed or fail, and yet be worth little or worth very much—nay more, he may be most fortunate or most miserable; no, his struggle is for good fortune and happiness itself.

What follows? In this competition, even if we give in for the moment, nothing prevents us from returning to the struggle; we have not to wait for another four years for the next Olympic Games to come. At once you may recover yourself, and pull yourself together, and renew the struggle with the same energy as before; and if you grow faint again, you may renew it again, and if you once attain to victory you are as one who has never failed. Only do not begin to take a pleasure in failing from sheer force of habit, and go about as a sorry athlete defeated in the whole round of all the Games, for all the world like quails that have escaped!

"I am overpowered by the impression of a pretty maid. Well! was I not overpowered lately? I am eager to find fault with some one. Did I not do so lately?"

You talk lightly to us, as though you had got off scot-free. It is as though a man, when his doctor forbade him to bathe, should say, "Why, did not I bathe quite lately?" What if the doctor can answer him, "Well, what effect did bathing have on you? Did you not fall into a fever? Did you not get a headache?" So when you found fault with some one lately, was it not the act of a bad man, and of a foolish one? Did you not feed this habit, by putting before it acts which were congenial to it? And when the pretty girl was too much for you, did you get away unpunished? What do you mean then by talking of what you did lately? Nay, you ought rather, I think, to have remembered, as slaves remember their floggings, and to have refrained from repeating the same offence. But it is not the same thing: pain makes the memory of the slave, but what pain or penalty attends your offences? When did you acquire the habit of avoiding evil activities?

CHAPTER 26: To Those Who Fear Want

Are you not ashamed of being more cowardly and mean-spirited than runaway slaves? How do they leave their masters when they run away? What lands or servants have they to trust to? Do not they steal just a morsel to last them for the first days, and then go on their way over land or it may be sea, contriving one resource after another to keep themselves alive? And when did a runaway slave ever die of hunger? Yet you are all of a flutter and keep awake at nights for fear you should run short of necessaries. Miserable man, are you so blind as not to see the road, to which want of necessaries leads you? Where does it lead? The same way as fever, the same way as a falling stone—to death. Well, and is not this exactly the situation you often described to your companions? Many a passage did you read and write about it. How often did you boast that you could face death at any rate with a quiet mind!

"Yes, but my family will starve."

What of that? Does their hunger lead in a different direction? Is not the way that leads below the same, and the world it leads to the same? Will you then not have courage to face every form of want and necessity, and to look on that world whither even the richest and those who have held the highest offices must descend, nay even kings and emperors themselves? Only you will descend hungry, if it so chance, and they will burst with over-eating and over-drinking.

Did you ever by chance see a beggar who was not old? They are all far gone in years; yet they bear the pinch of cold night and day, and lie forlorn upon the ground, and their food is what bare necessity demands and no more, but they almost arrive at immortality, and yet you who are sound in hand and foot are so afraid of starving!

Can you not draw water, or write, or take charge of children, or be another man's doorkeeper?

But it is disgraceful, you say, to be reduced to this necessity.

First learn then what is disgraceful, and then tell us that you are a philosopher; but for the present, if another call you so, do not allow him.

When a thing is not your business, when you are not responsible for it, when it has befallen you without your own act, like a headache or a fever, can it disgrace you? If your parents were poor, or if they made others their heirs instead of you, if they give you no help while they are alive, is this any disgrace to you? Is this what you learnt with the philosophers? Did you never hear that what is disgraceful is blameable, and the blameable is what deserves blame, and it is absurd to blame a man for what is not his own act, done by himself? Well, did you make your father what he is, or is it in your power to mend his character? Is this given you? What follows? Ought you to desire what is not given you, or to be ashamed if you do not attain to it? Is this all the habit you acquired when you studied philosophy, to look to others and to hope for nothing from yourself and your own acts? Lament therefore and mourn, and when you eat be fearful that you will have nothing to eat tomorrow. Tremble for your wretched slaves, lest they should steal, or run away, or die. Live in this spirit, and never cease to live so, you who never came near philosophy, except in name, and disgraced its principles so far as in you lies, by showing them to be useless and unprofitable to those who take them up. You never set your will to gain constancy, tranquillity, and peace of mind; you never paid regard to any master for this end, though you attended to many for the sake of syllogisms. You never tested any of these impressions thoroughly for yourself, asking, "Can I bear it or can I not? What have I to look to?" No, you assumed that all was well with you, and that you were quite secure, and devoted your efforts to the final study of all, how to be immovable. And in what were you to make yourself immovable? Cowardice, a base spirit, admiration of the rich, failure to get what you will, defeat of your will to avoid. It was to secure these results that you spent all your care.

Ought you not to win some possession from philosophy, before you try to make it secure? Did you ever see any one build a coping, unless he had a wall round which to build it? Who ever appoints a doorkeeper where there is no door to guard?

Again, you make it your study to be able to demonstrate. Demonstrate what? You study not to be shaken by fallacies. Shaken from what position? Show me first what you are guarding, what you are measuring, or what you are weighing; then it is time enough to show me the balance or the bushel. How long do you mean to measure dust and ashes? Ought you not to demonstrate those principles which make men happy, which make things prosper as they wish, principles which make them not blame any one or accuse any one, but acquiesce in the government of the universe? Show me these.

"See, I do show them," he says. "I will analyse syllogisms for you."

Slave, this is the measuring instrument, not that which is measured. That is why you now pay the penalty for your neglect of philosophy; you tremble, you lie awake, you take counsel with every one, and unless your plans promise to please every one you think you have taken bad counsel.

Then you fear starvation, as you think; but what you really fear is not starvation; you are afraid that you may not have a cook, that you may not have another to cater for you, another to shoe you, another to dress you, others to rub you, others to follow you; when you have stripped in the bath and stretched yourself out like the crucified, you want to be rubbed on this side and that, and then you want the masseur to stand by and say, "Turn, and give me his side, take his head, hand me his shoulder"; and then when you have left the bath and gone home you expect to cry out, "Will no one bring me something to eat?" and then, "Remove the tables, and wipe them." What you really fear is that you may not be able to live the life of an invalid; for the life of healthy men you have only to see how slaves and labourers and true philosophers live; the life of Socrates, though he had a wife and children to live with, the life of Diogenes, and of Cleanthes, who combined philosophy with drawing water. If this is what you want to have, you will have it everywhere, and will live with confidence. Confidence in what? In that which alone it is possible to confide in, what is trustworthy, and cannot be hindered or taken away, that is, your own will. Why have you made yourself so useless and unprofitable that no one is willing to take you into his house and take care of you? Every one will pick up a vessel that is whole and fit for use if it is flung aside and will count it gain; but every one will count you loss, not gain. Cannot you even serve the purpose of a dog or a cock? Why then do you wish to live any more, if this is your character?

Does a good man ever fear that food may fail him? It does not fail the blind, it does not fail the lame, will it fail the good man? There is no want of some one to give pay to the good soldier, or workman, or shoemaker: will the good man find none? Does God so disregard His own principles, His servants, His witnesses, whom alone He uses as examples to the untaught, to show "that He exists and orders the universe well, and does not disregard human things, and that for the good man nothing is evil, whether he lives or dies"? What if He does not provide food? It only means that, like a good general, He has given me the signal to retire. I obey, I follow, I praise my Commander, and laud His acts. For I came when He thought fit, and again shall go when He thinks fit; and while I lived this was the work I had to do, to praise God in my own heart, and to others, be it to one or to many. If He does not provide me with much or with abundance, His will is for me to live simply; for He did not give abundance to Heracles, His own son; another than he was king of Argos and Mycenae, and he was subject to him and suffered toils and discipline. Yet Eurystheus was the man he was, no true king of Argos and Mycenae, for he was not king over himself, while Heracles was ruler and commander of all land and sea, cleansing them from lawlessness and wrong, and bringing in justice and righteousness, and this he did unarmed and single-handed.

And when Odysseus was shipwrecked and cast ashore, his necessity never broke his spirit, or made it abject. Nay, how did he approach the maidens to ask of them the necessaries of life, which men think it most shameful to beg from another?

Like hill-bred lion, trusting in his might.

Trusting in what? Not in reputation, not in money, nor office, but in his own might, that is in judgements on things within our power and beyond it. For it is these alone that make free men, whom nothing can hinder, which lift up the neck of those who are in humiliation, and make them look with unwavering eyes upon rich men and upon despots.

And this was what the philosopher had to give, but you are going to leave him, it seems, not with courage but trembling for your pitiful clothes and plate. Miserable man! have you so wasted your time until now?

"What then, if I fall ill?"

You shall bear illness well.

"Who shall tend me?"

God, and your friends.

"I shall lie on a hard bed."
But you can do it like a man.
"I shall not have a proper house."
If you have one, you will be ill all the same.
"Who will give me food?"

Those who find it for others; you will be no worse off than Manes[1] on your sick-bed. And what is the end of the illness? Nothing worse than death. Will you realize once for all that it is not death that is the source of all man's evils, and of a mean and cowardly spirit, but rather the fear of death? Against this fear then I would have you discipline yourself; to this let all your reasonings, your lectures, and your trainings be directed; and then you will know that only so do men achieve their freedom.

---

[1] A slave's name. Epictetus uses the name and not the word "slave" because he does not wish to suggest a slave's spirit.

BOOK FOUR

CHAPTER 1: On Freedom

That man is free, who lives as he wishes, who is proof against compulsion and hindrance and violence, whose impulses are untrammelled, who gets what he wills to get and avoids what he wills to avoid.

Who then would live in error?

No one.

Who would live deceived, reckless, unjust, intemperate, querulous, abject?

No one.

No bad man then lives as he would, and so no bad man is free.

Who would live in a state of distress, fear, envy, pity, failing in the will to get and in the will to avoid?

No one.

Do we then find any bad man without distress or fear, above circumstance, free from failure?

None. Then we find none free.

If a man who has been twice consul hear this, he will forgive you if you add, "But *you* are wise, this does not concern you." But if you tell him the truth, saying, "You are just as much a slave yourself as those who have been thrice sold," what can you expect but a flogging?

"How can I be a slave?" he says; "my father is free, my mother is free, no one has bought me; nay, I am a senator, and a friend of Caesar, I have been consul and have many slaves."

In the first place, most excellent senator, perhaps your father too was a slave of the same kind as you, yes and your mother and your grandfather and the whole line of your ancestors. And if really they were ever so free, how does that affect you? What does it matter if they had a fine spirit, when you have none, if they were fearless and you are a coward, if they were self-controlled and you are intemperate?

"Nay, what has this to do with being a slave?" he replies.

Does it seem to you slavery to act against your will, under compulsion and with groaning?

"I grant you that," he says, "but who can compel me except Caesar, who is lord of all?"

Why, then, your own lips confess that you have one master: you must not comfort yourself with the thought that he is, as you say, the common master of all, but realize that you are a slave in a large household. You are just like the people of Nicopolis, who are wont to cry aloud, "By Caesar's fortune, we are free."

However, let us leave Caesar for the moment if you please, but tell me this: Did you never fall in love with any one, with a girl, or a boy, or a slave, or a free man?

"What has that to do with slavery or freedom?"

Were you never commanded by her you loved to do anything you did not wish? Did you never flatter your precious slave-boy? Did you never kiss his feet? Yet if any one compel you to kiss Caesar's, you count it an outrage, the very extravagance of tyranny. What is this if not slavery? Did you never go out at night where you did not wish, and spend more than you wished and utter words of lamentation and groaning? Did you put up with being reviled and shut out? If you are ashamed to confess your own story, see what Thrasonides says and does: he had served in as many campaigns or more perhaps than you and yet, first of all, he has gone out at night, at an hour when Getas does not dare to go, nay, if he were forced by his master to go, he would have made a loud outcry and have gone with lamentations over his cruel slavery, and then, what does he say?[1]

> *A worthless girl has made a slave of me,*
> *Whom never foe subdued.*

Poor wretch, to be slave to a paltry girl and a worthless one too! Why do you call yourself free then any more? Why do you boast of your campaigns? Then he asks for a sword, and is angry with the friend who refuses it out of goodwill, and sends gifts to the girl who hates him, and falls to praying and weeping, and then again when he has a little luck he is exultant. How can we call him free when he has not learnt to give up desire and fear?

Now look at the lower animals and see how we apply the notion of freedom to them. Men put lions in cages and rear them as tame creatures and feed them, and sometimes even take them about with them. Yet who will call a lion like that "free"? The softer he lives, the worse is his slavery. What lion, if he got sense or reason, would wish to be a lion

---

[1] Thrasonides and Getas are characters in Menander's play *Hated*.

of that sort? Look at the birds yonder and see what lengths they go in striving to escape, when they are caught and reared in cages; why, some of them actually starve themselves rather than endure that sort of life; and even those that do not die, pine away and barely keep alive, and dash out if they find any chance of an opening. So strong is their desire for natural freedom, an independent and unhindered existence.

Why, what ails you in your cage?

"What a question! I am born to fly where I will, to live in the air, to sing when I will; you take all this away from me, and say, 'What ails you?'"

Therefore we will call only those creatures free, that do not endure captivity, but escape by death as soon as they are caught. So too Diogenes says somewhere, "A quiet death is the one sure means of freedom," and he writes to the Persian king, "You cannot enslave the city of the Athenians any more than you can enslave fishes."

"What! shall I not capture them?"

"If you capture them," he says, "they will straightway leave you and be gone, like fishes; for when you take one of them, he dies. So if the Athenians die as soon as you take them, what is the good of your armament?" These are the words of a free man who has seriously examined the question and found the truth, as is reasonable; but if you look for it elsewhere than where it is, what wonder if you never find it?

The slave is anxious to be set free at once. Why? Do you think it is because he is anxious to pay the tax on his manumission? No! the reason is he imagines that up till now he is hampered and ill at ease because he has not got his freedom. "If I am enfranchised," he says, "at once all will be well, I heed nobody, I talk to all men as an equal and one of their quality, I go where I will, I come whence I will and where I will." Then he is emancipated, and having nothing to eat he straightway looks for some one to flatter and to dine with; then he either has to sell his body to lust and endure the worst, and if he gets a manger to eat at, he has plunged into a slavery much severer than the first; or if perchance he grows rich, being a low-bred fellow he dotes on some paltry girl and gets miserable and bewails himself and longs to be a slave again.

"What ailed me in those days? Another gave me clothes and shoes, another fed me and tended me in sickness, and the service I did him was a small matter. Now, how wretched and miserable I am, with many masters instead of one! Still, if I can get rings[2] on my fingers I shall live happily and prosperously enough."

And so first, to get them, he puts up with what he deserves, and

---

[2] The gold ring given to a freedman would open to him an official career as a knight.

having got them repeats the process. Next he says, "If I go on a campaign I am quit of all my troubles." He turns soldier and endures the lot of a criminal, but all the same he begs for a second campaign and a third.[3] Lastly, when he gets the crown to his career and is made a senator, once more he becomes a slave again as he goes to the senate; then he enjoys the noblest and the sleekest slavery of all.

Let him not be foolish, let him learn, as Socrates said, what is the true nature of everything, and not apply primary conceptions at random to particular facts. For this is the cause of all the miseries of men, that they are not able to apply their common primary conceptions to particular cases. One of us fancies this, another that. One fancies he is ill. Not at all; it is only that he does not apply his primary conceptions. Another fancies that he is poor, that his father or mother is cruel, another that Caesar is not gracious. But really it is one thing, and one thing only; they do not know how to adjust their primary conceptions. For who has not a primary notion of evil—that it is harmful, to be shunned, by every means to be got rid of? One primary notion does not conflict with another, the conflict is in the application.

What then is this evil which is harmful and to be shunned?

"Not to be Caesar's friend,"[4] he says.

He has gone out of his way, he has failed to apply his notions, he is in sore distress, he is seeking for what is nothing to the purpose; for when he has got Caesar's friendship he has equally failed of his object. For what is the object of every man's search? To have a quiet mind, to be happy, to do everything as he will, to be free from hindrance and compulsion. Very well: when he becomes Caesar's friend is he relieved from hindrance and compulsion, is he in peace and happiness? Of whom are we to inquire? Whom can we better trust than the very man who has become Caesar's friend?

Come forward and tell us! when was your sleep more tranquil, now or before you became Caesar's friend?

At once the answer comes, "Cease, by the gods I beg you, to mock at my fortune; you do not know what a miserable state is mine; no sleep comes near to me, but in comes some one to say, 'Now he's awake, now he'll be coming out'; then troubles and cares assail me."

Tell me, when did you dine more agreeably, now or before?

Hear again what he says about this: if he is not invited, he is distressed, and if he is invited he dines as a slave with his lord, anxious all the while for fear he should say or do something foolish. And what do you think he fears? To be flogged like a slave? How should he come off

---
[3] Three campaigns are a qualification for office.
[4] "Caesar's friend," a technical phrase for one who is received at Court.

so well? No, so great a man as he, and Caesar's friend, must fear to lose his neck; nought less were fitting. When did you bathe with more peace of mind, or exercise yourself more at your ease? In a word, which life would you rather live, today's or the old life? No one, I can swear, is so wanting in sense or feeling, that he does not lament his lot the louder the more he is Caesar's friend.

Inasmuch then as neither those who bear the name of kings nor kings' friends live as they will, what free men are left? Seek, and you shall find, for nature supplies you with means to find the truth. If, with these means and no more to guide you, you cannot find the answer for yourself, then listen to those who have made the search. What do they say?

Does freedom seem to you a good thing?

"The greatest good."

Can any one who attains the greatest good be miserable or fare badly?

"No."

Whensoever then you see men unhappy, miserable, mourning, you may declare with confidence that they are not free.

"I do declare it."

Well then, we have got away from buying and selling, and that kind of disposal of property which they deal with. For if you are right in making these admissions, no one who is miserable can be free, whether he be a great king or a little one, a consular or one who has twice been consul.

"Granted."

Answer me once more. Does freedom seem to you a great and noble and precious thing?

"Certainly."

Can then one who possesses so great and precious and noble a thing be of a humble spirit?

"He cannot."

Therefore when you see a man cringing to another or flattering him against his true opinion, you may say with confidence that he too is not free, and not only if he does it for a paltry dinner, but even if he does it for a province or a consulship. But those who do it for small objects you may call slaves on a small scale, and the others, as they deserve, slaves on a large scale.

"I grant you this too."

Again, does freedom seem to you to be something independent, owning no authority but itself?

"Certainly."

Then whenever a man can be hindered or compelled by another at will, assert with confidence that he is not free. Do not look at his grandfathers and great-grandfathers and search whether he was bought or sold, but if you hear him say "Master" from the heart and with feeling, then call him slave, though twelve fasces go before him;[5] and if you hear him say, "Wretched am I, that I am so treated," call him slave; in a word, if you see him bewailing himself, complaining, miserable, call him slave, though he wears the purple hem. If, however, he does not behave like this, call him not free yet, but get to know his judgements and see whether they are liable to compulsion or hindrance or unhappiness, and if you find any such, call him a slave on holiday at the Saturnalia;[6] say that his master is away; he will presently return and then you will learn his true condition.

"In what form will he return?"

In the form of every one who has authority over the things that a man wishes for, to get them for him or to take them away.

"Have we then so many masters?"

Yes, for even before these personal masters, we have masters in circumstance, and circumstances are many. It must needs follow then that those who have authority over any of these are our masters. For no one really fears Caesar himself; men fear death, exile, deprivation of property, prison, disfranchisement. Nor does any one love Caesar, unless he has great merit; we love wealth, the tribunate, the praetorship, the consulship. When we love and hate and fear these, the men who have authority over them are bound to be our masters, and that is why we worship them like gods; for we consider that that which has authority over the greatest benefit is divine; and then if we make a false minor premiss, "this man has control over the greatest benefit," our conclusion is bound to be wrong too.

What is it then which makes man his own master and free from hindrance? Wealth does not make him so, nor a consulship, nor a province, nor a kingdom; we must find something else. Now what is it which makes him unhindered and unfettered in writing?

"Knowledge of how to write."

What makes him so in flute playing?

"Knowledge of flute playing."

So too in living, it is knowledge of how to live. You have heard this as a general principle; consider it in detail. Is it possible for one who aims at an object which lies in the power of others to be unhindered? Is it possible for him to be untrammelled?

---

[5] The privilege of a consul.
[6] Festival of Saturn, December 17 and following days; one feature of it was that slaves were waited on by their masters.

"No."

It follows that he cannot be free. Consider then: have we nothing which is in our power alone, or have we everything? Or only some things in our power, and some in that of others?

"How do you mean?"

When you wish your body to be whole, is it in your power or not?

"It is not."

And when you wish it to be healthy?

"That is not in my power."

And when you wish it to be beautiful?

"That is not in my power."

And to live or die?

"That is not mine either."

The body then is something not our own and must give an account to any one who is stronger than ourselves.

"Granted."

Is it in your power to have land when you will, and as long as you will, and of the quality you will?

"No."

And slaves?

"No."

And clothes?

"No."

And your bit of a house?

"No."

And horses?

"None of these things."

And if you wish your children or your wife or your brother or your friends to live, whatever happens, is that in your power?

"No, that is not either."

Have you nothing then which owns no other authority, nothing which you alone control, or have you something of that sort?

"I do not know."

Look at the matter thus and consider it. Can any one make you assent to what is false?

"No one."

Well, then, in the region of assent you are unhindered and unfettered.

"Granted."

Again, can any one force your impulse towards what you do not wish?

"He can; for when he threatens me with death or bonds, he forces my impulse."

"Well now, if you despise death and bonds, do you heed him any longer?"
"No."
Is it your doing then to despise death, or is it not yours?
"Mine."
It rests with you then to be impelled to action, does it not?
"I grant it rests with me."
And impulse not to act, with whom does that rest? It is yours too.
"Supposing that my impulse is to walk, and he hinders me, what then?"
What part of you will he hinder? Your assent?
"No, but my poor body."
Yes, as a stone is hindered.
"Granted; but I do not walk any more."
Who told you that it is your business to walk unhindered? The only thing I told you was unhindered was your impulse; as to the service of the body, and its co-operation, you have heard long ago that it is no affair of yours.
"I grant you this too."
Can any one compel you to will to get what you do not wish?
"No one."
Or to purpose or to plan, or in a word to deal with the impressions that you meet with?
"No one can do this either; but if I will to get something a man will hinder me from obtaining it."
How will he hinder you, if you set your will upon things which are your own and beyond hindrance?
"Not at all."
But no one tells you that he who wills to get what is not his own is unhindered.
"Am I then not to will to get health?"
Certainly not, nor anything else that is not your own. For nothing is your own, that it does not rest with you to procure or to keep when you will. Keep your hands far away from it; above all, keep your will away, or else you surrender yourself into slavery, you put your neck under the yoke, if you admire what is not your own, and set your heart on anything mortal, whatever it be, or anything that depends upon another.
"Is not my hand my own?"
It is a part of you, but by nature a thing of clay, subject to hindrance and compulsion, slave to everything that is stronger than itself. Nay, why do I name you the hand? You must treat your whole body like a poor ass, with its burden on its back, going with you just so far as it may, and so far as it is given you; but if the king's service calls, and a soldier

Book Four

lays hands on it, let it go, do not resist or murmur; if you do, you will only get a flogging and lose your poor ass all the same.

But when this is your proper attitude to your body, consider what is left for you to do with other things that are procured for the body's sake. As the body is the poor ass, other things become the ass's bridle and pack-saddle, shoes and barley and fodder. Give them up too, let them go quicker and with a lighter heart than the ass itself.

And when you have prepared and trained yourself thus to distinguish what is your own from what is not your own, things subject to hindrance from things unhindered, to regard these latter as your concern, and the former as not, to direct your will to gain the latter and to avoid the former, then have you any one to fear any more?

"No one."

Of course. What should you fear for? Shall you fear for what is your own, that is, for what makes good and evil for you? Nay, who has authority over what is yours? Who can take it away, who can hinder it, any more than they can hinder God? Is it your body and your property that you fear for? Are you afraid for what is not your own, for what does not concern you at all?

Why, what have you been studying all along but to distinguish what is yours from what is not yours, what is in your power from what is not in your power, things subject to hindrance from things unhindered? Why did you go to the philosophers? Was it that you might be just as unfortunate and miserable as ever? I say that so trained you will be free from fear and perturbation. What has pain to do with you now, for it is only things that cause fear in expectation which cause pain when they come? What shall you have desire for any longer, for your will is tranquil and harmonious, set on objects within its compass to obtain, objects that are noble and within your reach, and you have no wish to get what is beyond your will, and you give no scope to that jostling element of unreason which breaks all bounds in its impatience?

When once you adopt this attitude towards things, no man can inspire fear in you any longer. For how can man cause fear in man by his aspect or his talk or by his society generally, any more than fear can be roused by horse or dog or bee in another horse or dog or bee? No, it is *things* which inspire fear in every man; it is the power of winning things for another or of taking them away from him, that makes a man feared.

How then is the citadel destroyed? Not by fire or sword, but by judgements. For if we pull down the citadel in the city, we have not got rid of the citadel which is held by fever or by fair women, in a word the citadel in ourselves and the tyrants who are within us, who threaten each one of us day by day, now in new forms, now in old. This is the point where we must begin, this is where the citadel must be destroyed, and the tyrants cast forth; we must give up our body, and all that belongs to it—faculties, property, reputation, offices, honors, children, brothers, friends—all these we must regard as having no concern for us.

If the tyrants are cast forth from this, what need is there for me to blockade the outward citadel? What harm does it do to me by standing? Why do I try and cast forth the guards? I feel them no longer; their rods and their spears and swords are pointed against others. I was never hindered in my will or compelled against my wish.

Nay, how can this be?

I have submitted my will[7] to God. He wills that I should have a fever; I will it too. He wills that I should have an impulse. I will it too. He wills that I should will to get a thing. I too will it. He wills that I should get something, and I wish it; He wills that I should not, I wish it no more. I am willing then (if He wills it) to die or be put on the rack. Who can hinder me any more against my own judgement or put compulsion on me? I am as safe as Zeus.

I act as the more cautious travellers do. A man has heard that the road is infested by robbers; he does not dare to venture on it alone, but waits for company—a legate, or a quaestor, or a proconsul—and joining him he passes safely on the road. The prudent man does the same in the world; in the world are many haunts of robbers, tyrants, storms, distresses, chances of losing what is dearest. "Where is a man to escape? How is he to go on his way unrobbed? What company is he to wait for that he may pass through in safety? To whom is he to join himself? To this or that rich man, or consular? What is the good of that? Your great man himself is stripped, and utters mourning and lamentation. What if my fellow traveller turns against me himself to rob me? What am I to do? I will be 'a friend of Caesar'; if I am his companion no one will do me wrong. But first, how many things must I endure and undergo, to become a distinguished person! How often must I suffer robbery and from how many! And then, if I rise to distinction, even Caesar is mortal. And if some circumstance lead him to become my enemy, where, I ask, is it better for me to retire? To the wilderness? Why, does not fever come there? What is to become of me then? Is it impossible to find a travelling-companion who is safe, trustworthy, strong, proof against attack?" Thus he reflects and comes to understand that if he attaches himself to God, he will pass through the world in safety.

"What do you mean by 'attach' himself?"

That what God wills, he may will too, and what God wills not, he may not will either.

---

[7] *Hormē*, "impulse," commonly used of the first step in a particular action, is here applied to the will in general.

Book Four

How then is this to be done?

How else, but by examining the purposes[8] of God and His governance of the world. What has He given me to be my own, and independent, what has He reserved for Himself? He has given me all that lies within the sphere of my choice, and has put it in my hands, unfettered, unhindered. How could He make my clay body free from hindrance? My property, my chattels, my honor, my children, my wife, He made subject to the revolution of the universe. Why then do I fight against God? Why do I will what is not for me to will, what is not given me to hold under all conditions, but to hold only as it is given and so far as it is given?

Suppose He that gave takes away. Why then do I resist? I shall not merely be silly, if I try to compel Him that is stronger; first of all I shall be doing wrong. For whence did I bring what I have into the world? My father gave them me. And who gave them him? Who is it that has made the sun, and the fruits of the earth, and the seasons, and the union and fellowship of men with one another?

You have received everything, nay your very self, from Another,[9] and yet you complain and blame the Giver, if He takes anything from you. Who are you and for what have you come? Did not He bring you into the world? Did not He show you the light? Has He not given you fellow workers? Has He not given you senses too, and reason? And in what character did He bring you into life? Was it not as a mortal, one who should live upon earth with his little portion of flesh and behold God's governance and share for a little while in His pageant and His festival? Will you not then look at the pageant and the festal gathering as long as it is given you, and then, when God leads you forth, go away with an obeisance to Him and thanksgiving for what you have heard and seen?

"No, I wanted to go on feasting."

Yes, those at the Mysteries too want to go on with the ceremony, and those at Olympia to see fresh competitors, but the festival is at an end. Leave it and depart, in a thankful and modest spirit; make room for others. Others must come into being, even as you did, and being born must have room and dwellings and necessaries. But if the first comers do not retire, what is left for them? Why will nothing satisfy or content you? Why do you crowd the world's room?

"Yes, but I want my wife and my children to be with me."

Are they yours? Are they not His who gave them? Are they not His who has made you? Will you not give up what is not yours, and give way to Him who is stronger than you?

---

[8] The will of God in its various manifestations.
[9] *I.e.*, God.

"Why then did He bring me into the world on these terms?"

Depart, if it does not suit you. God has no need of a querulous spectator. He needs men who join in the feast and in the dance, ready to applaud and glorify and praise the festival. But the impatient and miserable He will gladly see left outside the festival: for even when they were there they did not behave as at a festival nor fill the place appropriate to them, but were peevish and complained of fate and fortune and their company: insensible to fortune's gifts and to their own faculties, which they have received for just the opposite—a great heart, a noble spirit, and the very freedom we are now in search of.

"For what then have I received these gifts?"

To use them.

"For how long?"

Just so long as He who lent them wills.

"But what if they are necessary for me?"

Do not set your heart on them, and they will not be. Do not tell yourself that they are necessary, and they are not.

This is what you ought to practice from sunrise to sunset, beginning with the meanest things and those most subject to injury—a jug or a cup. From this go on to a tunic, a dog, a horse, a field; and from that to yourself, your body and its members, your children, your wife, your brothers. Look carefully on all sides and fling them away from you. Purify your judgements, and see that nothing that is not your own is attached to you or clings to you, that nothing shall give you pain if it is torn from you. And as you train yourself day by day, as in the lecture-room, say not that you are a philosopher (I grant you that would be arrogant), but that you are providing for your enfranchisement; for this is freedom indeed. This was the freedom which Diogenes won from Antisthenes, and said that no one could enslave him any more. That explains his bearing as a captive, and his behavior to the pirates: did he call any of them master? I do not mean the mere name (I have no fear of that), but the state of mind, of which it is the expression. Think how he rebukes them for feeding their prisoners badly. Think how he was sold: did he look for a master? No, for a slave.[10] And when he was sold, think how he bore himself towards his master: he began talking to him at once, telling him that he ought not to dress as he did, or shave as he did, and what life his sons ought to lead. What wonder in that? For if he had bought a slave skilled in gymnastic would he have used him as a servant in the palaestra or as a master? As a master; and in the same

---

[10] Menippus in "The Sale of Diogenes" says that when he was taken prisoner and sold he was asked what he could do. He answered, "Rule men," and to the auctioneer he said, "Does any one wish to buy himself a master?"

way if he had bought a man skilled in medicine or in architecture. And on this principle the man with skill is bound in every subject to be superior to the man without skill. Whoever then possesses knowledge of life in general must be master. For who is master on shipboard?

"The helmsman."

Why? Is it because any one who disobeys him is punished? No! but because he possesses skill in steering.

"But my master can flog me."

Can he do it with impunity?

"So I thought."

But as he cannot do it with impunity, therefore he has no authority to do it. No one can do wrong acts with impunity.

"What penalty falls on the man who imprisons his own slave, if he think fit?"

The very act of imprisoning him is his penalty, and this you will admit yourself, if you will hold fast the principle that man is not a brute but a civilized creature. For when does a vine do badly? When it acts against its nature. When does a cock do badly? In the same conditions. The same is true of a man. What is his nature then? Is it to bite and kick and cast into prison and behead? No, but to do good, to work with others and pray for them. Therefore, whether you will or no, man does badly when he acts without sense.

"Did not Socrates then do badly?"

No, but his judges and accusers did.

"Did not Helvidius[11] in Rome do badly?"

No, but his murderer did.

"What do you mean?"

Just as you do not say the fighting-cock has done badly when it has won and been wounded, but when it has been beaten without a scratch, and you do not count a hound happy when he does not strain in the pursuit, but when you see him sweating, in distress, his flanks bursting with the chase. What is there incredible in the statement that every man's evil is that which contradicts his nature? Is this incredible? Is it not what you say in every other sphere? Why then do you take another line only when man is in question? Is our other statement then incredible—that man's nature is civilized and affectionate and trustworthy?

"No, this is not, either."

How comes it then, further, that he suffers no harm though he be flogged or imprisoned or beheaded? Is not it true that, if he suffer these things in a noble spirit, he goes away the gainer, and is profited,

---

[11] Helvidius Priscus, son-in-law of Thrasea Paetus, whose Stoic principles he shared: put to death by Vespasian.

whereas he who suffers harm is the man who undergoes the most pitiful and shameful fate, the man who changes from a man into a wolf or a serpent or a wasp?

Come now and let us review the conclusions we have agreed to. He is free, whom none can hinder, the man who can deal with things as he wishes. But the man who can be hindered or compelled or fettered or driven into anything against his will, is a slave. And who is he whom none can hinder? The man who fixes his aim on nothing that is not his own. And what does "not his own" mean? All that it does not lie in our power to have or not to have, or to have of a particular quality or under particular conditions. The body then does not belong to us, its parts do not belong to us, our property does not belong to us. If then you set your heart on one of these as though it were your own, you will pay the penalty deserved by him who desires what does not belong to him. The road that leads to freedom, the only release from slavery is this, to be able to say with your whole soul:

> *Lead me, O Zeus, and lead me, Destiny,*
> *Whither ordainèd is by your decree.*

But, what say you, my philosopher, suppose the tyrant call on you to say something unworthy of you? Do you assent or refuse? Tell me.

"Let me think it over."

You will think it over now, will you? And what, pray, did you think over when you were at lecture? Did you not study what things are good and what are evil, and what are neither?

"Yes, I did."

What conclusion did you approve then?

"That things right and noble were good, things wrong and shameful bad."

Is life a good thing?

"No."

Is death evil?

"No."

Is prison?

"No."

And what did you think of ignoble and faithless speech, and treachery to a friend and flattery of a tyrant?

"We thought them evil."

Why do you ask the question now, then? You should have asked it and made up your mind long ago. It is nonsense to question now whether, when I can win the greatest goods, it is fitting for me not to win the greatest evils? A fine and necessary question forsooth, needing a deal of thought! Man, why do you mock us?

That is not the sort of thing that men "question." If you really imagined shameful acts to be bad, and noble acts good, and all else to be indifferent, you would not have proceeded to raise this question: not at all: you would at once have been able to decide the question by intuition, as an act of sight. For when do you question whether black things are white, or heavy things light, instead of following the obvious conclusions of your senses? Why then do you talk now of considering whether things indifferent are more to be shunned than things evil? These are not your judgements: prison and death do not seem to you indifferent, but the greatest evils, nor do base words and acts seem evil, they seem not to matter for us.

This is the habit to which you have trained yourself from the first. "Where am I? In the lecture-room. And who are listening to me? I am talking to philosophers. But now I have left the lecture-room. Away with those sayings of pedants and fools!" That is how a philosopher gives witness against a friend, that is how a philosopher turns parasite: that is how he hires himself out at a price, and speaks against his real opinion in the Senate, while in his heart[12] his judgement cries aloud, not a flat and miserable apology for an opinion, hanging to idle discussions as by a hair-thread, but a judgement strong and serviceable, trained by actions, which is the true initiation. Watch yourself and see how you take the news, I do not say that your child is dead (how should that befall you?), but that your oil is spilt, or your wine drunk up: well may one who stands by, as your temper rises high, say just this to you, "Philosopher, you use different language in the lecture-room: why do you deceive us? Why, worm that you are, do you call yourself a man?" I would fain stand by one of these men when he is indulging his lust, that I might see how eager he is, and what words he utters, and whether he remembers his own name, or the discourses which he hears or delivers or reads.

"Yes, but what has this to do with freedom?"

Nay! what else but this has to do with it, whether you rich people agree, or not?

"And who is your witness to this?"

Why, it is none other than your very selves. You who own that great master, and live at his nod and motion, and your blood runs cold if he so much as look at one of you with a sour face: you who pay court to old women and old men, and say, "I cannot do that, I am not allowed." Why are you not allowed? Did you not just now contend with me and assert you were free?

---

[12] Epictetus is describing the spurious philosopher, whose wisdom is only of the lecture-room, and whose real judgements "trained by actions" are revealed by his base conduct in the world.

"Yes, but Aprulla has forbidden me."

Tell the truth then, slave that you are, and do not run away from your masters, nor disown your slavery, nor dare to claim your enfranchisement, when you have so many proofs of slavery against you. I declare that the man who is compelled by love to act against his opinion, seeing the better course all the time, but wanting the strength to follow it, one might be more inclined to think deserving pardon, as overpowered by an influence violent and in a way divine. But who can bear with you, whose love is all for old women and old men, wiping their faces clean and washing them and giving them presents, and tending them like a slave in their illness, while all the time you are praying for them to die, and questioning the doctors, whether they are sick unto death at last? Or again, when you kiss the hands of other people's slaves in order to get those great and splendid offices and honors, becoming the slave of men who are not even free? Then, if you please, you walk in splendor as praetor or consul. Do I not know how you became praetor, where you got the consulship, who gave it you? For my part I would not wish to live, if I had to owe my life to Felicio,[13] and put up with his contempt and slavish arrogance; for I know what a slave is who is prosperous as the world thinks and puffed up with vanity.

"Are you then free?" says one.

By the gods, I wish to be and pray to be, but I cannot yet look in the face of my masters, I still set store by my poor body, I count it of great moment to keep it sound, yes though I have not a sound body to begin with. But I can show you one who is free, that you may not have to look for your example. Diogenes was free. How came he by this? Not because he was of free parents (he was not), but because he was free himself, had cast away all the weakness that might give slavery a hold on him, and so no one could approach or lay hold on him to enslave him. Everything he had he was ready to let go, it was loosely attached to him. If you had laid hold on his property, he would have let it go rather than have followed you for it; if you seized his leg, he would have let that go; if his whole poor body, he would have let his whole body go; and the same with kinsfolk, friends, and country. For he knew whence he had them and from whom, and on what conditions he received them. His true ancestors, the gods, and his true Country he would never have deserted, nor have suffered another to yield them more obedience or attention, nor would another have died for his Country more cheerfully. For he never sought to get the reputation of acting for the universe, but he remembered that everything that comes to pass has its source there and is done for that true Country's sake and is entrusted to us by Him

---

[13] Name used for the type of an influential slave.

that governs it. Wherefore look what he says and writes himself: "Therefore, Diogenes," he says, "you have power to converse as you will with the king of the Persians and with Archidamus,[14] king of the Lacedaemonians." Was it because he was the son of free parents? When all the men of Athens and Lacedaemon and Corinth were unable to converse with them as they wished, and feared and flattered them instead, was it because they were sons of slaves? "Why have I the power to do it then?" he says. "Because I count my poor body not my own, because I need nothing, because law and nothing else is all in all to me." These were the things which left him free.

And that you may not think that I point you to the example of a man alone in the world, with no wife or children or country or friends or kindred, who might have bent his will and drawn him from his purpose, take Socrates and look at him: he had wife and children, but regarded them as not his own; a country, in such manner and so far as duty allowed: friends, kinsmen, all these things he had made subject to law and obedience to law. For this reason, when duty called him to take the field, he was the first to leave Athens and ran all risks of battle most ungrudgingly, but when he was sent by the Tyrants to fetch Leon,[15] he never entertained the idea, because he thought it shameful, though he knew that he would have to die, if it so chanced. And what did it matter to him? Why, he wanted to preserve something else—not his poor flesh, but his honor and self-respect. These are things which cannot be trusted to another or made subject to another. Afterwards when he had to plead for his life, did he behave as one who had children or as one who had a wife? No, but as one alone in the world. And again, when he had to drink the poison, how did he behave? When he might have saved himself, and when Crito said to him, "Escape, for the sake of your children," what did he say? Did he think the chance a godsend? No, he looked at what was fitting, and had no eye, no thought for anything besides. For he wished to save not his poor body, but "that which right increases and preserves, and wrong diminishes and makes to wither." Socrates refuses to save himself with dishonor: he who would not put the question to the vote, when the Athenians bade him, who despised the Tyrants, who held such noble discourse on virtue and goodness—it is impossible to save him with dishonor: his safety is secured by death, not by flight. For the good actor too, if he stops when he ought, has more chance of safety than one who acts out of season.

What will your children do then?

---

[14] King of Sparta, 361–338 B.C.
[15] Leon of Salamis, whom Socrates was ordered by the Thirty Tyrants to arrest.

"If I had gone away to Thessaly you would have looked after them: and when I have gone away to Hades, will there be no one to look after them?"

See how he calls death by smooth names and scoffs at it. But if you and I had been in his place, we should at once have argued that we ought to repay injury with injury: and we should have added, "I shall be useful to many men if I keep alive, but to no one if I die." Nay, had it been necessary to creep out through a hole in the rock to escape, we should have done so. And yet how could we have been of use to any one? For those we were trying to help would not have stood fast.[16] Or again, if we did good by living, should we not have done much more good to men by dying when and as we ought? Even so now that Socrates is dead, the memory of what he did or said in his lifetime is no less useful to men, or it may be even more useful than before.

Make this your study, study these judgements, and these sayings: fix your eyes on these examples, if you wish to be free, if you set your desires on freedom as it deserves. It is no wonder that you pay this great, this heavy price for so vast an object. Men hang themselves, or cast themselves down headlong, nay sometimes whole cities perish for the sake of what the world calls "freedom," and will you not repay to God what He has given, when He asks it, for the sake of true freedom, the freedom which stands secure against all attack? Shall you not practice, as Plato says, not death only, but torture and exile and flogging, in a word practice giving back all that is not yours? If not, you will be a slave among slaves, even if you are consul ten thousand times, and no less, if you go up into Caesar's Palace; and you will discover that "what philosophers say may be contrary to opinion," as Cleanthes said, "but not contrary to reason." For you will really get to know that what they say is true, and that none of these objects that men admire and set their hearts on is of any use to those who get them, though those who have never chanced to have them get the impression, that if only these things were theirs their cup of blessings would be full, and then, when they get them, the sun scorches them and the sea tosses them no less, and they feel the same boredom and the same desire for what they have not got. For freedom is secured not by the fulfilling of men's desires, but by the removal of desire. To learn the truth of what I say, you must spend your pains on these new studies instead of your studies in the past: sit up late that you may acquire a judgement that makes you free: pay your attentions not to a rich old man, but to a philosopher, and be seen about his doors: to be so seen will not do you discredit:

---

[16] The meaning seems to be that by their bad example in clinging to life they would demoralize those whom they were trying to help.

you will not depart empty or without profit, if you approach in the right spirit. If you doubt my word, do but try: there is no disgrace in trying.

CHAPTER 2: On Intercourse with Men

The one thing to be careful about beyond all others is this—not to get so involved with any of your former companions or friends, as to compromise your character for his sake, for if you do this you will destroy yourself. If the thought slips in, "I shall seem rude to him, and he will not be the same to me as before," remember that nothing is done without paying for it, and that it is not possible to be the same man that you once were, unless you do as you did before. Choose then which you will—to be like your former self and be loved as before by those who loved you, or to be better than before, and so miss what they once gave you. For if this is the better choice, then incline to this, and let no irrelevant arguments distract you, for no one can make progress by facing both ways. No; if you have chosen this course before all, if you wish to devote yourself to this and nothing else, and to spend all your labour on this, then dismiss all other thoughts, or else this facing both ways will produce a double result—you will not make progress as you ought, and you will fail to get what you got before; for before, when you frankly set your desires on worthless objects, you were agreeable to your companions. You cannot excel both ways; in proportion as you succeed on the one side, you must needs fall short on the other. When you do not drink with those whom you used to drink with, you cannot seem as agreeable to them as of old; choose then, whether you wish to be a drinker and gratify them, or sober and displease them. If you do not sing with those that you sang with, you cannot win their affection as before: here too then you must choose which you prefer. For if it is better to have self-respect and self-control, than to have it said of one, "What a charming fellow!", then give up all other considerations, put them from you, turn away from them, and have nothing to do with them. But if this is not going to satisfy you, then turn round completely, and practice the very opposite—unnatural lust, adultery, and all that is in keeping with them, and you shall get what you want. Yes, jump up and shriek applause over your dancer.

But characters so opposite do not mix: you cannot act both Thersites and Agamemnon. If you want to be Thersites you must be humpbacked and bald, if Agamemnon, you must be handsome and tall, and love your subjects.

CHAPTER 3: What to Aim at in Exchange

If you give up any external possession, mind you see what you are to get in exchange for it: and if it is worth more, then never say, "I have been a loser." You will not lose if you get a horse for an ass, an ox for a sheep, a noble action for a piece of money, true peace instead of pedantry, self-respect instead of foul language. If you remember this you will everywhere preserve your character as it ought to be: if you do not remember it, I warn you that your time perishes for nought, and you will waste and overthrow all the pains that you now spend upon yourself. It needs but a little to overthrow and destroy everything—just a slight aberration from reason. For the helmsman to wreck his vessel, he does not need the same resources, as he needs to save it: if he turn it but a little too far to the wind, he is lost; yes, and if he do it not deliberately but from mere want of attention, he is lost all the same. It is very much the same in life: if you doze but a little, all that you have amassed up till now leaves you. Keep awake then and watch your impressions: it is no trifle you have in keeping, but self-respect, honor, constancy, a quiet mind, untouched by distress, or fear, or agitation—in a word, freedom.

What are you going to sell all this for? Look and see what your purchase is worth.

"But I am not going to sell my freedom for anything of that kind."[1]

Well, suppose you waive external gain, consider what the exchange is that you are making. It is yours to say, "Self-control for me, a tribunate for him: a praetorship for him, self-respect for me. I do not clamor, when to do so is unseemly, I will not jump from my seat, when I ought not, for I am free and God's friend, to obey Him of my own free will. I must not lay claim to anything else—body, property, office, reputation, anything in short, for He does not wish me to lay claim to them: had He wished it, He would have made them good for me, but He has not done so, and therefore I cannot transgress any of His commands." In everything you do, guard what is your own good: for the rest, be content just to take anything that is given you, so far as you may use it rationally. Otherwise you will be wretched and miserable, hampered and hindered. These are the laws that are sent you from God, these are His ordinances. These you must expound, and these obey, not those of Masurius and Cassius.[2]

---

[1] *I.e.*, anything external.
[2] Famous lawyers of the first century A.D.

CHAPTER 4: To Those Whose Heart Is Set on a Quiet Life

Remember that it is not only desire of office and of wealth that makes men abject and subservient to others, but also desire of peace and leisure and travel and learning. Regard for any external thing, whatever it be, makes you subservient to another. What difference does it make then whether you desire to be a senator, or not to be a senator, to be in office, or to be out of office? What difference is there between saying, "I am miserable, I don't know what to do, I am tied to my books like a corpse," and saying, "I am miserable, I have no leisure to read"? For books, like salutations and office, belong to the outer world which is beyond your own control. If you deny it, tell me why do you want to read? If you are drawn by the mere pleasure of reading, or by curiosity, you are a trifler, without perseverance: but if you judge it by the true standard, what is that but peace of mind? If reading does not win you peace of mind, what is the good of it?

"Nay," he says, "it does, and that is just why I am vexed at being deprived of it."

And what, pray, is this peace of mind, which any one can hinder—I do not mean Caesar, or Caesar's friend, but a raven, a flute-player, a fever, countless other things? Nothing is so characteristic of peace of mind as that it is continuous and unhindered. Suppose now I am called away to do something: I shall go and attend to the limits which one must observe—acting with self-respect and security, with no will to get or to avoid external things, watching men also to see what they say and how they move, and that not from ill nature, nor to blame or mock at them, but looking at myself all the time to see if I am making the same mistakes too.

"How then shall I cease [to err]?" you ask.[1]

Time was when I made the same mistakes as others, but I do so no more, thanks be to God. If you have acted thus and devoted yourself to this, have you done worse than if you had read a thousand lines or written as many? When you eat, are you vexed that you are not reading? Are you not content with eating as your reading bids you? And the same when you wash and take exercise? Why, then, do you not keep an equable tenor always, even when you approach Caesar or this or that great man? What do you lack, if you keep yourself free from passion, undismayed, modest, if you are rather a spectator of events than a

---

[1] The connection of this sentence with the preceding is not clear. I have tried to make sense by dividing it between the student who asks what is the good of attending to one's conduct, and Epictetus who answers that God has helped him to escape from error, and his pupil may escape in the same way.

spectacle to others, if you do not envy those preferred to you, if you are not dazzled by material things?

You say you lack books? How, or to what end? Books are, no doubt, a preparation for life, but life itself is made up of things different from books. To ask for books is as though an athlete should complain, as he enters the arena, that he is not training outside. Life is what you were training for all along, this is what the leaping-weights, and the sawdust, and the young men you wrestled with were leading up to. What? Are you hankering after them, when the time for action is come? It is as if in the sphere of assent, when impressions are presented to us, some which are "apprehensive," and some which have no such power, we should refuse to distinguish between them and should prefer to read the theory of apprehensive impressions.[2]

What, then, is the reason of our failure?

The reason is that we never directed our reading or our writing to the right object—that is, to dealing naturally with the impressions that come upon us, when we have to act. We are content to go thus far and no farther—to understand what is said, and to be able to explain it to another, to analyse the syllogism and trace out the hypothetical argument. Therefore hindrance besets us in the sphere where our pains are spent.

Do you want things which are not always in your power?

Be condemned, then, to hindrance, obstruction, failure. But if we were to study the doctrine of impulse, not to see what is said about impulse but to make our own impulses good, if we were to study the will to get and the will to avoid to the end that we may never fail to get what we will nor fall into what we avoid, and study the doctrine of what is fitting that we may remember our true relations and may do nothing irrationally or contrary to what is fitting—then we should not have to suffer vexation at being hindered in regard to the principles we have studied, but should find contentment in acting in accordance with them, and we should cease to calculate as we have been wont to do till today, "Today I read so many lines, wrote so many," and should reckon thus, "Today I governed my impulse by the precepts of the philosophers, I did not entertain desire, I avoided only things within the compass of my will, I was not awed by this man, or over-persuaded by that man, but trained my faculty of patience, of abstinence, of co-operation": and then we should give thanks to God, for the gifts for which our thanks are due.

As it is, we do not realize that we too, with a difference, behave like the multitude. Another man fears that he may not become a magis-

---

[2] "Apprehensive impressions." See note 1 on page 17.

trate, you fear that you may be one. Man, act not so. Nay, just as you laugh at him who fears he may not hold office, so laugh at yourself too. There is nothing to choose between being thirsty with fever, and shunning water like a madman. If you act thus, how shall you be able to say, as Socrates did, "If God so wills, so be it?" Do you think that, if Socrates had set his desire on a life of leisure and daily conversation with young men in the Lyceum or the Academy,[3] he would have cheerfully gone on all the campaigns in which he served? Would he not have groaned and lamented, "Unhappy that I am, wretched and miserable in the field, when I might be sunning myself in the Lyceum." What? Was this your task in life, to sun yourself? Was it not to have a mind at peace, to be free from hindrance and encumbrance? Nay, how would he have been Socrates any more, if he had lamented like that? How could he have written songs of triumph in prison?

In a word, then, remember this, that, whenever you pay regard to anything outside your will's control, you so far destroy your will. And freedom from office lies outside your will just as much as office, leisure just as much as business.

"Am I, then, to pass my life amid this tumult?"

What do you mean by "tumult"?

"Amid a multitude of men."

Well, and what is there hard in that? Imagine you are at Olympia, make up your mind that it is a festival. There, too, one cries this, another that, one does this, another that, and one man jostles another. The public baths, too, are thronged, yet which of us does not enjoy this assemblage, and leave it with pain? Be not dissatisfied nor peevish at what happens. "Vinegar disgusts me, for it is acid; honey disgusts me, for it upsets my tone; I dislike green stuff." In the same way you say, "I dislike retirement, it means solitude; I dislike a crowd, it means disturbance."

Say not so, but, if things so turn out, that you live alone or in a small company, call it "peace" and make a proper use of it: converse with yourself, train your impressions, develop your primary notions. If you chance on a crowd, call it "games," "assembly," "festival," and try to share the feast with your fellow men. For what sight is pleasanter for the man who loves his kind than a multitude of men? We are pleased to see troops of horses or oxen, we delight to see a multitude of ships: does the sight of a multitude of men vex us?

---

[3] Lyceum, a gymnasium northeast of Athens, a haunt of Socrates; Academia, a gymnasium in the northwest of Athens, where Plato taught.

"Nay, but their clamor overwhelms me."

Well, that is only a hindrance to your hearing: how does it affect you? Does it affect your faculty of dealing with your impressions? Who can hinder you from dealing naturally with the will to get and the will to avoid, the impulse to act and not to act? What tumult can avail to touch these?

Only remember these general principles: "What is mine, what is not mine? What is given me? What does God wish me to do now? What does He not wish?" A little while ago His will was that you should live a quiet life in converse with yourself, and write on these matters, read, listen, prepare yourself: you had sufficient time for this. Now He says to you, "Now come into the conflict, show us what you have learnt, how you have trained. How long are you going to exercise yourself in solitude? The time has now come for you to discover whether you are an athlete worthy of victory, or one of those who go about the world suffering continual defeat." Why, then, are you vexed? There is no conflict without a crowd: there must be many to train beforehand, many to cry applause, many stewards, many spectators.

"Yes, but I wanted to live a quiet life."

Lament and mourn, then, as you deserve: for what greater penalty than this can fall on him who is uninstructed and disobedient to the ordinances of God than to be distressed, to mourn, to envy, in a word, to be unhappy and miserable? Have you no wish to free yourself from these ills?

"And how shall I free myself?"

Have you not often heard, that you must get rid of the will to get altogether, and must will to avoid only those things which are within your control? That you must give up everything—body, property, reputation, books, the throng, office, private life? For if once you swerve from this path you become a slave and a subject, you are liable to hindrance and compulsion, and completely at the mercy of others. But the saying of Cleanthes is ready to our need,

Lead me, O Zeus, and lead me, Destiny.

Will you have me go to Rome? To Rome then. To Gyara? I will go to Gyara. To Athens? I will go to Athens. To prison? I will go to prison. If once you say, "When are we to get away to Athens?" you are lost. That wish, if unfulfilled, must make you miserable, and, if fulfilled, it must make you puffed up, elated on false grounds: again, if you are hindered, it must make you unhappy, at the conflict between circumstances and your will. Give up all these things then.

"Athens is beautiful."

Yes, but happiness is far more beautiful—freedom from passion and disturbance, the sense that your affairs depend on no one.

"In Rome there is crowd and salutations."

Yes, but peace of mind outweighs all discomforts. If, then, the time for these has come, why do you not get rid of your will to avoid them? Why must you bear your burden like a cudgelled ass? If you do this, you must needs (look you) be the perpetual slave of him who has power to accomplish your departure, or him who can in any way hinder it, and you are bound to pay respect to him as to an Evil Genius.

There is but one way to peace of mind (keep this thought by you at dawn and in the daytime and at night)—to give up what is beyond your control, to count nothing your own, to surrender everything to heaven and fortune, to leave everything to be managed by those to whom Zeus has given control, and to devote yourself to one object only, that which is your own beyond all hindrance, and in all that you read and write and hear to make this your aim. Therefore I cannot call a man industrious, if I am merely told that he reads or writes, no, not even if one adds "he is at work all night," unless I know what he is working for. You do not call a man industrious who keeps late hours for the sake of a mistress: neither do I. But if he does it for glory, I call him ambitious; if for money, I call him fond of money, not fond of work. But if the object of his work is his own Governing Principle, if he is working to make this live a natural life, then and then only I call him industrious. You must never praise or blame men for qualities that are indifferent, but for their judgements. For it is these which are each man's property, these which make their actions base or noble. Bear this in mind and rejoice in what is at hand and be content with what the moment brings. If you see any of the principles that you have learnt and thought over being realized by you in action, rejoice over them. If you have put away bad nature, and evil-speaking, or made them less, if you have got rid of wantonness, foul speaking, recklessness, slackness, if you are not excited by things that once excited you, or at least not as before, then you can keep festival day by day, today because you behaved well in this action, tomorrow because you did well in another. How much greater cause is this for offering sacrifice than if you were made consul or prefect! These things come to you from your own self and from the gods. Remember Who is the Giver, and to whom He gives and why. If you are brought up to reason thus, you need no longer raise the question, "Where shall I be happy?" and "Where shall I please God?" Do not men have their equal portion in all places? Do they not everywhere alike behold what comes to pass?

CHAPTER 5: To Those That Are Contentious and Brutal

The good and noble man does not contend with any one, and to the best of his power does not suffer others to contend. We have an illustration of this, as of other qualities, set out for us in the life of Socrates, who not only avoided contention himself on all occasions, but tried to prevent the contentions of others. Look at the *Symposium* of Xenophon and see how many contentions he has reconciled, and again how patient he was with Thrasymachus, with Polus, with Callicles,[1] and how patient always with his wife, and with his son, when his son tried to convict him of fallacious arguments. For he remembered to hold fast the truth that no man is master of another's Governing Principle. Therefore he wished to do nothing that was not his own. What does that mean? Not to move other people to act naturally, for that is not his to do: but to let others act for themselves, as they think fit, and himself none the less to live and spend his days in accord with nature, only doing his own business in such a way that they, too, should follow nature. For this is the conduct which the good and noble man always has set before him.

Is it his will to become praetor?

No: but if this is given him, to keep his own Governing Principle in these circumstances.

To marry?

No, but if marriage is given him, to keep himself in a natural state in those circumstances. But if he wills that his son or his wife should not go wrong, then he wills to make his own what is not his own. In fact education is this, to learn what is one's own and what is not.

Where, then, is there any room for contention if a man bears himself thus? Is he amazed at anything that happens? Does anything take him by surprise? Does he not expect the wicked to deal worse and more severely with him than the event turns out? Does he not count everything gain in which they fall short of the worst?

"Such a one reviled you."

Many thanks to him for not striking.

"But he did strike too."

Many thanks to him for not wounding.

"But he did wound."

Many thanks to him for not killing. For when, or in whose school,

---

[1] Thrasymachus, the famous sophist of Chalcedon, often mentioned by Plato; Polus, a Sicilian sophist of the fifth century B.C. and a character in Plato's *Gorgias*; Callicles, a character in *Gorgias*, who advocates the free life of uncontrolled passions.

did he learn "that man is a gentle and sociable creature and that wrongdoing in itself does great harm to the wrongdoer"?

If, then, he has not learnt this or been convinced of it, why should he not follow what appears to be his interest?

"My neighbor has thrown stones."

Is that any offense on your part?

"But my crockery is broken."

You are no piece of crockery: you are a rational will. You ask what is given you to meet this attack? If you want to act the wolf, you may bite back, and throw more stones at him than he threw: but if you seek to act as a man, then examine your store and see what faculties you have brought into the world with you. Have you brought the faculty of a brute, the faculty of revenging wrongs? When is a horse miserable? When it is deprived of its natural faculties, not when it is unable to crow like a cock, but when it is unable to run. And the dog? Not when it cannot fly, but when it cannot follow a trail. On the same principle a man is wretched, not when he cannot throttle lions or embrace statues[2] (for he has not been endowed by nature with faculties for this), but when he has lost his rational and trustworthy faculty. This is he for whom men

> *should meet and mourn*
> *The miseries he has come to,*

not, by Zeus, the man who is born or dies, but he whose lot it is to lose while he lives what is his own—not his patrimony, his paltry field or house or inn or slaves (for none of these is man's own, but all are alien to him, all are subject and subservient to their Masters, who give them now to one now to another)—to lose the qualities that make him man, the distinctive stamp impressed upon his mind: like the stamp we look for on coins, which if we find we pass them, and if we do not, fling them away.

Whose imprint does this sesterce bear?

"Trajan's."[3]

Here with it.

"Nero's."

Fling it away, it will not pass, it is good for nothing.

So, too, it is with man. What stamp have his judgements? "Gentle, sociable, patient, affectionate." Good, I accept him, I make him a citizen, I accept him as a neighbor and fellow voyager. Only beware that he has not the stamp of Nero. Is he hot-tempered, is he wrathful, is he

---

[2] *Cf.* III. 12, note 1.
[3] Trajan, Emperor A.D. 98–117.

querulous? "If it takes his fancy, he cuffs the heads of those he meets." Why, then, did you say that he is a man? Is everything judged by its outward form alone? On that principle you must call your waxen apple an apple. No, it must smell and taste like an apple: the outward semblance is not enough. So, when you judge man, nose and eyes are not sufficient, you must see if he has the judgements of a man. Here is one who does not listen to reason, does not understand when his fallacies are exposed; he is an ass. Here is one whose self-respect is deadened: he is useless, anything rather than a man. Here is one looking to find some one he can kick or bite; it follows he is not even a sheep or an ass, but some savage beast or other.

"What then? Do you want me to be despised?"

By whom? By those who know? Nay, how will those who know despise one who is gentle and self-respecting? By those who do not know? What do you care for them? No craftsman cares for those who have no skill!

"Yes, but they will attack me much more."

What do you mean by "me"? Can any one injure your will or hinder you from dealing with the impressions you meet with in a natural way?

"No."

Why, then, do you persist in being troubled and want to show yourself a man of fears? Why do you not come forward and openly proclaim that you are at peace with all men, whatever they do, and that you laugh above all at those who think that they are harming you? saying, "These slaves do not know who I am, nor where to find what is good or bad for me, for they have no way of getting at my position." In the same way those who inhabit a strong city laugh at those who besiege it. "Why are these men troubling themselves for nothing? Our wall is secure, we have food for a long time, and all other supplies." These are the things that make a city secure against capture; the soul of man is made secure by judgements alone. For what wall is so strong, or what substance so impenetrable, or what property so secure against robbery, or what reputation so unassailable? When the objects that a man sets his mind on are bound to bring him trouble of mind, sick hopes, fear, mourning, disappointment of the will to get, failure of the will to avoid, they are always subject to death and to capture.

If this be so, are we not willing to make the one means of safety which is given us secure, and, abandoning what is mortal and slavish, to spend our efforts on what is immortal and free by nature? Do we not remember that one man does not harm nor benefit another? It is man's judgement on each situation that harms him. It is this which overthrows him, this is contention, this is faction, this is war. The conflict of Eteocles and Polynices[4] was caused by nothing else but this judgement, the judgement on kingship, the judgement on exile—that exile is the worst of evils, kingship the greatest good: and the nature of every man is this—to pursue the good, to avoid the evil, to consider him who takes away from one's good and who involves one in evil as an enemy and aggressor, even though he be a brother, a son, a father, for no kinship is closer than that of the good. Wherefore, if these outward things are reckoned good and evil, there is no love between father and sons or between brother and brother, but the whole world is full of enemies, aggressors, malicious persons. But if a right will is the only good thing, and a wrong will the only evil, what becomes of conflict and reviling? How can it arise? Over things that do not concern us? With whom should we contend? With the ignorant, the miserable, with those who are deluded in regard to the highest matters?

Socrates remembered this when he lived in his own house and bore with a most shrewish wife and an unfeeling son. For what did her shrewishness mean? Pouring water at will over his head, and trampling on his cake. What is that to me, if I make up my mind that it is nothing to me? This is what I have to do, and no king nor master shall hinder me against my will, the many shall not prevail against the one, nor the stronger against the weaker: for God has given each man his reason to use unhindered. These judgements make affection in a household, concord in a city, peace among nations; they make a man grateful towards God, confident in all places, for he looks on outward things as alien to him and as worth nothing. But though we are capable of writing and reading these sentiments, though we can praise them as we read, yet they do not bring conviction to us, nor anything like it. Wherefore the proverb about the Lacedaemonians,

Lions at home, foxes at Ephesus,

will fit us too. In the lecture-room we are lions, and foxes in the world outside!

CHAPTER 6: To Those Who Are Distressed at Being Pitied

"I am vexed," he says, "at being pitied."

Is it your doing that you are pitied, or the doing of those who pity you? Or again, does it rest with you to stop their pity?

"Yes, if I show them that I do not deserve their pity."

---

[4] The two legendary sons of Oedipus, whose quarrel over the government of Thebes led to the expedition of "The Seven against Thebes."

But is it in your power, or is it not, not to deserve pity?

"I think that it is in my power."

But these men do not pity you for what would deserve pity, if anything did—I mean for your errors—but for poverty and lack of office and diseases and death and other things of this sort. Are you, then, prepared to persuade the multitude that none of these things, after all, is evil, but that it is possible for a man who is poor, and without office or honor, to be happy, or do you try to show off to them as a man of wealth and office? The second course stamps you as a braggart without taste or worth. And consider by what means you would achieve your pretence: you will have to borrow some wretched slaves and possess a few pieces of plate, and show them many times over, if you can, and try not to let men know that they are the same; and you must display gay apparel and other splendors and show yourself off as one who is honored by eminent persons and must try to dine at their table, or at least be thought to do so; and you must use base arts on your person, to make yourself seem handsomer and better made than you really are: these are the contrivances you must adopt, if you wish to take the second way of avoiding pity.

But the first way is a long, nay an endless, one—to attempt the very task which Zeus could not accomplish—to convince all men of what is good and what is evil. Is this given to you? No! This only is given you—to convince yourself: you have not yet done that: and yet you are already attempting—are you?—to convince others. Why! who has been your companion so long as you have been yourself, and who can exercise such persuasion on you as you can on yourself, and who is more kindly and friendly disposed to you than you are? How is it, then, that you have not yet persuaded yourself to learn? Are not your thoughts turned upside down? Have you set your mind on this, and not on learning how to be quit of pain and trouble and humiliation, and so to be free? Have you not heard, then, that there is but one way which leads to this—to give up all that lies beyond the will, to abandon it and confess that it is not yours?

To what class of things does another man's opinion about you belong?

"To what is outside the will."

Then it concerns you not at all?

"Not at all."

While, then, you still allow yourself to be vexed and troubled at men's opinion, do you imagine that you have attained conviction as to what is good and evil?

Will you not, then, let other men alone and become your own master and pupil? "Other men shall see for themselves whether it is to their advantage to be in an unnatural state and live their lives so, but no man is nearer me than I am myself. Why is it, then, that though I have heard the arguments of philosophers and assent to them, they have not lightened my burden? Am I so wanting in ability? Why, in all the other things I chose to undertake, I was not found to be duller than most. I was quick at learning letters and wrestling and geometry and the analysis of syllogisms. Is it, then, that reason has failed to convince me? Why, there is nothing which I have so stamped with my approval and choice from the first—and even now these principles are the subject of my reading, I hear and write of nothing else: up till today we have found no argument to prevail against this. What then do I lack? Is it that the contrary judgements have not been removed from my mind? Is it that my own convictions are untrained and unaccustomed to confront facts, like arms put away in a cupboard and grown rusty, that cannot be fitted to my body? Yes, of course! In wrestling or writing or reading I am not content with merely learning; I twist the arguments put before me to and fro and construct new ones, and I deal with variable premisses in like manner. But when I have to deal with those necessary principles, which enable a man, if he grounds himself on them, to escape pain, fear, passion, hindrance—to be free, I do not exercise myself in them nor devote to them the practice that is proper for them. And then, am I concerned by what the multitude will say of me, and whether in their eyes I shall appear a happy or important personage?"

Miserable man, will you not see what opinion you pronounce on yourself? How do you appear to yourself? What manner of man in thought, in will to get and will to avoid: what manner of man in impulse, preparation, design, and the other activities of man? Yet you are concerned whether other men pity you?

"Yes, but they pity me when I do not deserve it."

Is this what pains you? and is the man who is pained to be pitied?

"Yes."

Then you are not pitied without deserving it after all. By the very feelings you entertain in regard to pity you make yourself worthy of pity. What does Antisthenes say? Did you never hear? "It is the part of a king, Cyrus, to do well and be ill-spoken of." My head is sound and all think that I have a headache. What do I care? I am free from fever, and men sympathize with me as though I had fever: "Unhappy man, this long time you have had fever without ceasing." I put on a gloomy face and assent: "It is quite true I have been ill for a long time." "What is to happen then?" "What God wills": and as I say it I laugh in my sleeve at those who pity me.

What prevents me, then, from doing the same here too? I am poor, but I hold a right judgement on poverty: what do I care then, whether they pity me for poverty? I am not in office and others are; but I hold the right opinion as to being in office and out of it. Those who pity me shall take their own views: I have neither hunger nor thirst nor cold, but their own hunger or thirst makes them imagine the same of me. What am I to do for them then? I go about proclaiming and saying, "Sirs, be not deluded, all is well with me, I take no heed of poverty, or want of office, or, in a word, of anything at all except right judgements: these I hold free from hindrance, I have paid regard to nothing besides." Yet what nonsense am I talking? How do I hold right judgements any longer if I am not content with being what I am, and am excited over other men's opinion of me?

"But others will get more than I do, and will be preferred to me."

Well, what is more reasonable than that those who have spent their pains on any object should have the advantage in that on which they have spent their pains? They have spent their pains on office, you on judgements, they on wealth, you on the way to deal with impressions. See whether they have the advantage of you in that on which you have spent pains and which they neglect: whether in assent they keep more to natural standards, whether they are more successful in getting what they will to get, and in avoiding what they will to avoid, whether in design, in purpose, in impulse they aim better than you, whether they do what is fitting for them as men, as sons, and as parents, and in each relation that you name in turn. But if they hold office and you do not, will you not tell yourself the truth—that you do nothing to gain office, and they do everything, and it is most unreasonable that one who pays attention to a thing should have less success in it than one who does not?

"Nay, but I pay regard to right judgements and therefore it is more reasonable that I should rule."

Yes, in judgements, for you have devoted yourself to them: but you must give place to others in that to which they have devoted themselves. You might as well claim to be a better shot with the bow than regular bowmen because you have right judgements, or to be better at smith's work than the professional smith. Give up your devotion to judgements then and busy yourself with the objects you wish to obtain, and then complain if you do not succeed, for you have a right to complain. But, as it is, you say you are bent on other things, and attending to other things, and the proverb of the people is a good one: "One business has nothing in common with another." One man rises at dawn and tries to find whom he can salute as he leaves home, or to whom he can make a pleasant speech, or send a gift, how he can please the dancer, how he can deal maliciously with one man to gratify another. When he prays, his prayers are for this object; when he sacrifices, his sacrifice is for this; the prayer of Pythagoras[1]—

That sleep fall not upon his tender eyes—

he has turned to this end. "How went I wrong?" Was it in matters of flattery? "What wrought I?" Have I acted as a free man and a gentleman? And if he finds himself acting so he blames and accuses himself, and says, "Whatever should you say this for? Might you not have told a lie? Even philosophers say, 'There is nothing to hinder one's telling a lie.'"

But if you have really given your mind to nothing but how to deal properly with impressions, then as soon as you get up in the morning you must consider, "What do I lack to secure freedom from passion? What do I lack to be unperturbed? What am I? am I a mere body, or property, or reputation?"

None of these.

What then?

A rational creature.

What then are the demands upon me?

Reflect upon your actions. "Where have I gone wrong" in regard to peace of mind? "What have I done" unfriendly, or unsociable, or heartless? What did I fail to accomplish in this regard that I ought to have done?

Seeing then that there is this great difference in men's desires and acts and prayers, do you still wish to be equal with them in matters to which they have given their minds and you have not? And, that being so, are you surprised and annoyed if they pity you? They are not annoyed if you pity them. Why? Because they are convinced that their lot is a good one, and you are not convinced. That is why you are not content with your portion, but hanker after theirs, and they are content with their portion and do not hanker after yours. For, if you were really convinced that you are right in regard to what is good and that they are far away from the truth, you would never have taken any account of what they say of you.

CHAPTER 7: On Freedom from Fear

What makes the Emperor an object of fear?

The guards, one says, with their swords, and the chamberlains and those who close the door against those who enter.

Why is it then that, if you bring a child to him when his guards are

---

[1] Pythagoras, of Samos, one of the earliest Greek philosophers (*flor.* 540–510 B.C.).

with him, the child is not afraid? Is it because the child is not aware of them? Now if a man is aware of the guards and their swords, but comes for that very purpose, because his misfortunes make him wish to die and he is anxious to die easily by some one else's hand, does he fear the guards?

"No, for he wishes for the very thing which makes men fear them."

If then a man whose will is not set on dying or living, but who is content with what is given him, comes before the Tyrant, what prevents him from coming without fear?

"Nothing."

Now suppose a man is of the same mind in regard to property as this man in regard to his body: suppose he feels the same about wife and children: suppose, in a word, he is so distracted and desperate that he regards it as indifferent whether he has these things or not: just as children playing with potsherds are anxious about the game, but do not care for the potsherds in themselves, so he has not set his heart on material things, but accepts the game cheerfully, and enjoys handling them—how can any tyrant, how can any guards or swords inspire fear in such a one?

Yet if madness can produce this attitude of mind, if even habit can produce it in the Galilaeans,[1] can reason and demonstration teach no one that God has made all things in the world, and the world itself as a whole to have its own end without hindrance, but its individual parts to subserve the whole? Now all other things are without the capacity of understanding His governance, but the rational creature has faculties that enable him to reflect on all these things, to realize that he is a part, and what part he is, and that it is well for the parts to give way to the whole. And further, being by nature noble and generous and free, he sees that he has some of the things about him unhindered and in his own control, and some again subject to hindrance and dependent on others, the acts of his will unhindered, and things beyond his will subject to hindrance. And therefore if he makes up his mind that his good and his interest lie in the former alone, in things that are unhindered and depend upon himself, he will be free, tranquil, happy, unharmed, high-minded, reverent, giving thanks for everything to God, on no occasion blaming or accusing any one for what happens; but if he finds his good in things outside and beyond his will, he is bound to be hindered and hampered, and to be the slave of those who have authority over those things on which his admiration and his fear are centered, he is bound to be irreverent because he thinks that God is injuring him,

---

[1] *I.e.*, Christians.

and unfair, always seeking to win for himself more than his share; he is bound to be of a mean and paltry spirit.

If a man understands this, there is nothing to prevent him from living with an easy and obedient spirit, content with his past lot and awaiting with a gentle spirit all that may yet befall him.

"Would you give me poverty?" Give it me and you shall learn what poverty is when a good actor plays the part. "Would you give me office?" Give it me, and troubles with it. "Exile?" Wherever I go, it will be well with me: for even here it was not the place that made me well off, but my judgements, and these I shall carry away with me, for no one can rob me of them; these alone are my own and cannot be taken away, with these I am content wherever I am and whatever I do. "But now the time is come to die." What do you mean by "die"? Do not use fine words, but state the facts as they are. "Now is the time for your material part to be restored to the elements of which it was composed." What is there dreadful in that? What loss to the universe will this mean, what strange or irrational event? Is this a thing to make one fear the tyrant? Is this what makes the swords of the guards seem long and sharp? Let others look to that; I have considered the whole matter, and no one has authority over me. God has set me free, I have learnt to understand His commands, no one can make a slave of me any more, my judges and he who claims my freedom[2] are as they should be.

"Am I not master of your body?"

What does that concern *me*?

"Am I not master of your property?"

Well, how does that concern *me*?

"Am I not master of exile and imprisonment?"

Again, I resign all, yes, and my body itself for you to deal with, when you will. Only try your authority and you will learn how far it extends. What then can I fear any more? The chamberlains? What should I fear their doing? Fear their shutting me out? If they find me wanting to enter, let them shut me out!

"Why then do you come to the king's door?"

Because I think it is fitting for me to join in the game while it lasts.

"How then do you escape being shut out?"

If I am not received, it is not my will to enter; my will is always to prefer what comes to pass, for I consider what God wills better than what I will. I will attach myself to Him as His minister and servant, my impulses and my wishes are one with His, in a word my will is His will. There can be no exclusion for me, but only for those who try to press in.

---

[2] *Cf.* III. 24, note 4.

Why then do I not press in?

Because I know that nothing good is given within to those who have entered. But when I hear a man called happy because he is honored by Caesar I say, "What is his portion?" "A province or a procuratorship." Does he also get a judgement, such as a governor should have? Does he get the skill to use a procuratorship? Why should I push my way in any more? Some one flings a shower of figs and nuts: the children try to seize them, and fight with one another for them; grown men do not, for they count it a small matter. If one fling potsherds even children do not try to catch them. Governorships are being given to this man and that: the children shall see to them! A praetorship, a consulship: let the children scramble for them: let them be shut out and beaten, let them kiss the hands of the giver and his slaves; for me they are figs and nuts. But what if a fig chance to fall into my lap when he is throwing? Take and eat it, for one may value a fig so far. But if I stoop for it and upset my neighbor or am upset by him, if I flatter those who enter, the fig is not worth while, nor is any other of the good things which the philosophers have persuaded me not to believe to be good.

Show me the swords of the guards.

"See how large and how sharp they are."

Well, what do these large, sharp swords do?

"They kill."

What does fever do?

"The same."

What does a tile do?

"The same."

Would you have me then stand in awe of all these things, and pay them reverence, and go about as the slave of all?

God forbid! No, if I have once learnt that what is born must needs also be destroyed in order that the world may not stand still or be hindered, it makes no difference to me whether a fever is to destroy it or a falling tile or a soldier, but if I must compare them I know that the soldier will do the thing quicker and with less pain. Seeing then that I neither fear anything that he can do to me nor desire anything that he can provide, why do I stand in awe and amazement before him any more? Why do I fear the guards? Why do I rejoice if he speaks to me in a friendly way and gives me a welcome? Why do I tell other people how he talked to me? Is he a Socrates or a Diogenes, that his praise of me should be a proof of what I am? Do I admire his character? No, it is to keep up the game that I come to him and serve him, so long as he commands me to do nothing stupid or unseemly. But if he says to me, "Go and fetch Leon of Salamis," I say to him, "Look for some one else, I will play no longer."

"Away with him."

I follow; it is in the game.

"But you lose your neck."

Well! does the Emperor himself, and you who obey him, keep his neck for ever?

"But you will be flung abroad unburied."

I shall be, if I and the dead body are one, but if I am not the same as the dead body, state the facts with more discrimination, and do not try to frighten me. These are things to frighten children and fools. But if a man has once entered a philosopher's lecture-room and does not know what his true self is, he deserves to fear and to flatter what he flattered afterwards: I mean, if he has not yet learnt that he is not flesh or bones or sinews, but the faculty which uses them, and which also governs the impressions and understands them.

"Yes, but these arguments make men despise the laws."

Nay, these arguments of all others make those who adopt them obedient to the laws. Law is not what any fool can do. Yet see how these arguments make us behave rightly even towards our critics, since they teach us to claim nothing against them, in which they can surpass us. They teach us to give way in regard to our poor body, to give way in regard to property, children, parents, brothers, to give up everything, resign everything: only our judgements they reserve, and these Zeus willed should be each man's special property. How can you call this lawlessness, how can you call it stupidity? I give way to you in that wherein you are better and stronger than I: where, on the other hand, I am the better man, it is for you to give way to me, for I have made this my concern, and you have not. You make it your concern, how to live in a palace, how slaves and freedmen are to serve you, how you are to wear conspicuous raiment, how you are to have a multitude of huntsmen, minstrels, players. Do I lay claim to any of these? But you, for your part, have you concerned yourself with judgements? Have you concerned yourself with your own rational self? Do you know what are its constituents, what is its principle of union, how it is articulated, what are its faculties and of what nature? Why are you vexed then, if another who has made these things his study has the advantage of you here?

"But these are the greatest matters of all."

Who, I ask, prevents you from busying yourself with these and devoting your attention to these? Who has a larger equipment of books, of leisure, of masters who will do you good? Only incline your mind to these things, bestow a little time, if no more, on your own Governing Principle, consider what this possession is and whence it has come to you, this faculty which uses all the rest, which proves all the rest, selecting and rejecting. So long as you busy yourself with external things, no one will succeed with them so well as you, but this faculty of reason will be, what your own choice makes it, moldy and neglected.

CHAPTER 8: To Those Who Hastily Assume the Character of Philosophers

Never bestow praise or blame on any one for qualities which are indifferent, nor credit them with skill or want of skill; then you will escape at once from recklessness and malice. "This man washes hastily." Does he do evil then? Not at all. What is it he does then? He washes hastily. Do you mean that everything is well done? By no means: but acts based on right judgements are done well and those based on bad judgements are done badly. Until you have learnt from what judgement each of a man's acts proceeds, do not praise or blame him. But a judgement is not easily determined by externals. "This man is a carpenter." Why? "He uses an adze." What has that to do with it? "This man is a musician, for he sings." What does that matter? "This man is a philosopher." Why? "He wears a cloak and long hair." But what do mountebanks wear? Therefore, if a man sees one of them misbehaving, he says at once, "Look what the philosopher is doing." But his misconduct should rather have led him to say that he was no philosopher. For, if this is the primary conception and profession of a philosopher, to wear a cloak and long hair, they would be right: but if it is rather this—to be free from error—why do they not deprive him of the name "philosopher" because he does not fulfil the philosopher's profession? For this is what happens in other arts. When one sees a man planing badly, one does not say, "What is the good of the carpenter's art, see what bad work carpenters do," but one says quite the contrary, "This man is not a carpenter, for he planes badly." In like manner if one hears a man singing badly, one does not say, "See how badly musicians sing," but rather, "This man is no musician." It is only in regard to philosophy that men behave so: when they see any one acting contrary to the philosopher's profession, instead of refusing him the name, they assume that he is a philosopher, and then finding from the facts that he is misbehaving, they infer that there is no use in being a philosopher. What is the reason for this? The reason is that we pay regard to the primary notion of the carpenter, and to that of the musician, and to that of other craftsmen in like manner, but pay no regard to the notion of the philosopher, but as it is indistinct and inarticulate in our minds we judge it by externals only. Can you name any other art that is acquired by dress and hair, and is destitute of principles and subject-matter and end?

What then is the subject-matter of the philosopher? Is it a cloak?

No, it is reason.

What is his end? Is it to wear a cloak?

No, but to keep his reason right.

What are his principles? Are they concerned with how to grow a long beard or thick hair?

No, but rather, as Zeno says, to understand the elements of reason, the true nature of each, and how they are duly related to one another, and all that is consequential on this. Will you not, then, first see whether he fulfils his profession by behaving unseemly, and only then, if it be so, accuse his calling? As it is, when you think that he is behaving ill, when your own conduct is discreet, you say, "Look at the philosopher," as though it were fitting to call the man who acts so a philosopher, and again, "There's your philosopher!" But you do not say, "Look at the carpenter," or "Look at the musician," when you discover one of that class in adultery or see him eating greedily. So true it is that you realize the philosopher's profession to a certain extent, but you fall away from it and are confounded by sheer want of practice.

But even those who are called philosophers use vulgar means to pursue their calling: they just put on a cloak and let their beard grow and say, "I am a philosopher." But no one if he merely buys a harp and a plectrum will say, "I am a musician," nor if he puts on a smith's cap and apron will say, "I am a smith": no doubt they fit the dress to the art, but they take their name from the art and not from the dress. For this reason Euphrates was right in saying, "For a long time I tried not to be known for a philosopher and this was useful to me. For, in the first place, I knew that what I did rightly was done for my own sake and not for the spectators: it was for myself that I ate rightly and was modest in my aspect and my gait: all was for myself and God. Secondly, as the performance was mine only, so also was the risk: if I did anything shameful or unseemly the cause of philosophy was not endangered, nor did I injure the public by going wrong as a philosopher. For this reason those who did not know my design wondered how it was that, though I was familiar and conversant with all philosophers, I was not a philosopher myself. What harm is there in the philosopher being discovered by my acts, and not by outward signs?"

See how I eat, how I drink, how I sleep, how I bear and forbear, how I work for others, how I exercise the will to get and the will to avoid, how I observe my relationships, natural and acquired, without confusion and without hindrance. Judge me by this, if you can. But if you are so deaf and blind, that you do not consider Hephaestus a good smith unless you see him with his smith's cap on his head, what harm is there in being unrecognized by so foolish a judge?

So it was that most men did not recognize Socrates for a philosopher, and they came to him and asked him to introduce them to philosophers. Well, was he annoyed with them, as we should be? Did he say, "Do not you think me a philosopher?" No, he took them and introduced them, and was content with this one thing, that he was a philosopher, and was glad that he was not vexed at being not taken for one: for he remembered his proper business.

What is the business of a good and true man? To have many pupils?

Certainly not: those who have set their heart on that shall look to that. Is it then to take difficult principles and define them precisely?

Others there will be who will look to this.

Where then was it that Socrates asserted himself and wished to assert himself?

In the region of injury and benefit. "If any one," said he, "can injure me, I am of no good; if I wait for some one to benefit me, I am naught. If I will, and my will is not done, I am miserable." This was the great field of conflict[1] to which he challenged every man, and in which I think he would have given way to none. But how, think you? Was it by proclaiming aloud, "This is the man I am"? Never! but by being the man he was. For, again, it is a fool's and a braggart's part to say, "I am free from passion and tumult. Men, I would have you know, that, while you are in turmoil and disturbance about worthless matters, I alone am relieved from all perturbation." What, are you not content to be free from pain, without proclaiming, "Come, all ye who suffer from gout, headache, fever, come ye lame and blind and behold how I am untouched by any sickness"? That is a vain and vulgar boast, unless, like Asclepius,[2] you can at once show them by what treatment they too can be relieved of disease, and for this purpose produce your own good health as an example.

Such is the character of the Cynic whom Zeus has deemed worthy of crown and scepter. He says, "Men, you are looking for happiness and peace not where it is but where it is not, and, that you may see this, behold I have been sent to you by God as an example, having neither property nor house nor wife nor children—no, not even a bed or a tunic or a piece of furniture. See how healthy I am. Try me, and if you see that I am at peace in my mind, hear my remedies and the treatment which cured me." This indeed is a humane and noble saying. But notice whose work it is: the work of Zeus or whomsoever He thinks worthy of this service—never to lay bare before the multitude any weakness whereby he should make of none effect the witness which he bears to virtue, and bears against outward things.

---

[1] *Skamma*, a pit made for wrestlers or jumpers.
[2] Aesculapius, the god of healing.

> *His noble face ne'er paled, nor from his cheeks*
> *Wiped he a tear.*

Not only so, he must not long for anything or hanker after anything—human being or place or way of life—as children hanker after sweet grapes or holidays: he must be adorned with self-respect on every side, as others find their adornment in walls and doors and doorkeepers.

Instead of that your would-be philosophers just take a start towards philosophy, and, like dyspeptics rushing to some dainty food, of which they are bound soon to grow sick, they claim at once the scepter and the kingdom. He lets his hair grow, assumes a cloak, bares his shoulder for all to see, fights with those that meet him, and, if he sees any one in a fine cloak, quarrels with him. Man, discipline yourself first: watch your own impulse, to see that it is not like the sickly craving of a woman with child. Study first not to let men know what you are: keep your philosophy to yourself for a little. That is how fruit is produced. The seed must needs be buried first, and be hidden, and increase by slow degrees, that it may come to fullness. But if it bear the ear before it grows the stalk, it is like a plant from the garden of Adonis[3] and comes to no good. That is the sort of plant you are: you have blossomed sooner than you ought, and will wither away when the storm comes.

Look what farmers say about seeds, when the hot weather comes before its time. They are all anxiety for fear that the seeds should grow insolent and then a single frost seize them and expose their weakness. You, too, man, must beware: you have grown insolent and have leapt to an opinion before the time: you think yourself a somebody, fool that you are among fools; you will be frost-bitten, nay you are frost-bitten already down at the root, though above you still blossom for a little and therefore think you are still alive and flourishing. Leave us at least to ripen in the natural course. Why do you expose us to the air, why do you force us? We cannot bear the air yet. Let the root grow, and then produce the stem, first one joint, then the second, then the third: then in that way the fruit will force its way naturally, whether I will or no.

For who that has conceived and travailed with such great judgements does not become aware of his own gifts and hasten to act in accordance with them? Why, a bull is not ignorant of his own nature and endowment when he catches sight of a wild beast, nor does he wait for some one to encourage him; and so with a dog, when he sees a wild animal. If then I have the equipment of a good man, am I to wait for you to equip me to do my proper work? But as yet I have not the

---

[3] Garden of Adonis: plants grown in a pot for the festival of Adonis: used of transitory things.

equipment, believe me. Why then would you make me wither away before the time, just as you have withered away yourself?

CHAPTER 9: To One Who Was Modest and Has Become Shameless

When you see another man in office, set against his office the fact that you have no need of office: when you see another rich, look what you have instead. If you have nothing instead, you are miserable, but if you have this—that you have no need of wealth—know that you are better off and have something much more valuable. Another has a beautiful wife, you have freedom from desire for a beautiful wife. Do these seem to you small matters? Nay, what a price the rich themselves, and those who hold office, and who live with beautiful wives, would give to despise wealth and office and the very women whom they love and win! Do you not know what the thirst of a man in a fever is like, how different from the thirst of a man in health? The healthy man drinks and his thirst is gone: the other is delighted for a moment and then grows giddy, the water turns to gall, and he vomits and has colic, and is more exceeding thirsty. Such is the condition of the man who is haunted by desire in wealth or in office, and in wedlock with a lovely woman: jealousy clings to him, fear of loss, shameful words, shameful thoughts, unseemly deeds.

"Nay, but what do I lose?" he says.

Man, you were self-respecting and are so no more; have you lost nothing? Instead of Chrysippus and Zeno you read Aristides and Evenus;[1] have you lost nothing? Instead of Socrates and Diogenes you admire the man who can cajole and corrupt most women. You want to be handsome and you make yourself up as what you are not; you want to show off glittering clothes, that you may attract women's eyes, and you count yourself lucky if you light on some precious cosmetic. Before, you thought of none of these things; your only concern was to find seemly discourse, a man of worth, a noble thought; and therefore you slept like a man, you walked like a man, you dressed like a man, your conversation was what a good man's should be. Can you say then, "I have lost nothing"? Do you mean that men lose nothing but mere money? Is there no loss of self-respect, no loss of decency? Does the loss of these count for nothing? To you perhaps the loss of these qualities seems as nothing: there was a time when you counted this the only loss

---

[1] Aristides of Miletus, supposed author of licentious "Milesian tales" of the Alexandrian period. Evenus of Paros, a writer of elegiac poems (about 460–390 B.C.).

and the only harm, and when your one anxiety was that no one should dislodge you from these views and these acts.

And lo! you have been dislodged from them, but by none other than yourself. Fight against yourself, deliver yourself, that you may be modest, self-respecting, free. If any one ever told you that some one was compelling me to be a profligate, to dress like a profligate, to scent myself, would you not go and murder the man who so abused me? Will you not help yourself then? And how much easier this help is to give! There is no need to kill or to imprison or to assault any one, no need to come out into the market-place: you have only to talk to yourself, to the man who is most likely to be persuaded, and whom no one can persuade better than yourself. Therefore, first realize what is happening to you, and having done so, do not be faint-hearted or behave as men of a mean spirit do, who when once they have given in surrender completely and are swept away, so to speak, by the stream: no, learn a lesson from the trainers. The boy has fallen, suppose. "Get up," says the trainer, "and wrestle again, until you are made strong." Let this be your attitude; for know that nothing is more amenable than the mind of man. You have but to will a thing and it is done, and all is right; on the other hand you have but to relax your effort and all is lost. For destruction and deliverance lie within you.

"What good do I get then?"

What greater good do you look for than this? You were shameless and shall be self-respecting, you were undisciplined and shall be disciplined, untrustworthy and you shall be trusted, dissolute and you shall be self-controlled. If you look for greater things than these, go on doing as you do now: not even a god can save you.

CHAPTER 10: What Things We Should Despise, and What We Should Deem Important

All men's difficulties and perplexities are concerned with external things. "What am I to do?" "How is it to be done?" "How is it to turn out?" "I fear this or that may befall me." All these phrases are used by persons occupied with matters outside their will. For who says, "How am I to refuse assent to the false?" "How am I to refuse to swerve from the true?" If a man is so gifted by nature as to be anxious about these things, I will remind him: "Why are you anxious? It rests with you: be not troubled. Be not over-hasty in assent, before you have applied the rule of nature."

Again, if he is anxious about his will to get, lest it should fail of its object and miss the mark, and about his will to avoid, lest it should fall into what it avoids, first of all I will salute him, because he has got rid of the excitements and fears of other men, and has turned his thoughts to his own business where his true self lies. Then I shall say to him: "If you would not fail to get what you will, nor fall into what you will to avoid, do not will to get what is not your own, nor to avoid what is not in your control: otherwise you are bound to fail and to fall into disaster. Where is the difficulty if you do as I say? What room is there for phrases like, 'How am I to get it?' 'How is it to turn out?' 'I fear this or that may befall me.'

Is not the issue of the future outside our will?

"Yes."

And the essence of good and evil is in the region of the will?

"Yes."

Is it in your power then to make a natural use of every event that happens? Can any one hinder you from that?

"No one."

Say no more then, "What is to happen?" For whatever happens, you will turn it to good purpose, and the issue will be your good fortune. What would Heracles have been if he had said, "How am I to prevent a big lion from appearing, or a big boar, or brutal men?" What care you, I say? If a big boar appears, you will have a greater struggle to engage in; if evil men appear, you will free the world from evil men.

"But if I die thus?"

You will die a good man, fulfilling a noble action. For since you must die in any case, you must be found doing something—whatever it be—farming or digging or trading or holding the consulship or suffering indigestion or diarrhoea. What then would you have death find you doing? For my part I would be found busy with some humane task, whatever it be—something noble, beneficent, advancing the common weal. And if I cannot be found doing great things like these, I would do what none can hinder, what is given me to do, setting myself right, bringing to perfection the faculty that deals with impressions, working to achieve freedom from passion, rendering what is due to each relation in life; nay, if I am so fortunate, attaining to the third sphere of activity, that concerned with certainty of judgements.

If death finds me thus occupied, I am content if I can lift up my hands to God and say, "I have not neglected the faculties which I received from Thee, to enable me to understand Thy governance and follow it, I have not dishonored Thee so far as in me lay. See how I have dealt with my senses, see how I have dealt with my primary notions. Did I ever complain of Thee, did I ever show discontent with anything that happened to any one, or wish it to happen otherwise, did I offend in my relations towards others? In that Thou didst beget me I am grateful for Thy gifts: in so far as I have used what Thou gavest me I am satisfied. Take Thy gifts back again and place them where Thou wilt: for they were all Thine, Thou hast given them to me." Are you not content to leave the world in this state of mind? Nay, what life is better or more seemly than his who is so minded, and what end can be more happy?

But to achieve this, you must put up with great troubles and great losses. You cannot have this and wish to get a consulship, you cannot have this and set your heart on owning lands, you cannot take thought for yourself and for wretched slaves at the same time. No, if you wish for what is not your own, you lose what is yours. This is in the nature of things: nothing is done but at a price. And what need for wonder? If you wish to become consul, you must keep late hours, run to and fro, kiss people's hands, lie perishing at other men's doors, say and do many things unfit for a free man, send gifts to many, and presents every day to some. And what do you get for it? Twelve bundles of rods,[1] the privilege of sitting three or four times on the tribunal and of giving games in the Circus, and doles in baskets. If it be not so, let any one show me what there is besides. Will you then spend nothing, and use no effort to secure release from passion and perturbation, that sleeping you may sleep and waking you may wake, that you may fear nothing and be anxious for nothing? But if while you are thus engaged you have losses or spend money amiss, or if another gets what you ought to have got, are you going to be vexed all at once at what happens? Will you not weigh what the exchange is and how precious your gain, instead of wishing to obtain this great prize for nothing? Nay, how can you? "One business interferes with another."

You cannot combine attention to outward possessions with attention to your own Governing Principle. If you want outward things, let your reason go, or you will have neither the one nor the other, being pulled both ways. If you wish for reason, you must let outward things go. The oil will be spilt, my poor furniture will perish, but I shall be free from passion. Say a fire shall arise when I am away and my books perish, yet I shall deal with my impressions in accord with nature.

"But I shall have nothing to eat."

If I am so miserable, death is my harbor. Death: this is the harbor, this the refuge from all things, therefore nothing in life is difficult. When you wish, you leave, and no smoke annoys you. Why then are you anxious, why keep late hours? Why do you not reckon up at once where your good and your evil lie, and say, "Both are in my power: no one can deprive me of my good, and no one can plunge me in evil against my will. Why then do I not snore at my ease? I am secure in

---

[1] The 12 fasces (bundles of rods with axes) were the mark of a consul.

what is mine: what is not mine will be the concern of any one who gets it as a gift from Him who has authority to give it. Who am I to will that what is not mine should be thus or thus? Is it given to me to choose? Has any one set me to administer it? I am content with the things over which I have authority. These I must make as beautiful as possible; the rest must be as their master wills."

If a man has this before his eyes he is no longer wakeful, "hither and thither tossed." What would he have, or what does he long for? Does he long for Patroclus or Antilochus[2] or Menelaus? When did he think any of his friends was immortal? When had he not before his eyes the fact that tomorrow or the day after he or his friend must die?

"Yes," he says, "but I thought he would outlive me and enrich my son."

Yes, for you were a fool, and set your thoughts on uncertainties. Why then do you not accuse yourself, instead of sitting crying like young girls?

"Nay, but he set food for me to eat."

Yes, fool, for he was alive: now he cannot. But Automedon[3] will set meat for you, and if he dies you will find another. If the pot in which your meat was boiling is broken, must you needs die of hunger, because you have lost the pot you are used to? Do not you send and buy another?

"Nay," he says,

"No worse ill could befall me."

What! Is this what you call ill? And yet you forbear to remove it and blame your mother for not warning you, that you might spend your days lamenting ever since. What think you? Did not Homer compose these lines on purpose that we might see that there is nothing to prevent the noblest, the strongest, the richest, the most handsome, from being most wretched and most miserable when they have not the judgements they should have?

CHAPTER 11: On Cleanliness

Some men raise the question whether the social faculty is a necessary element in man's nature: nevertheless even they, I think, would not question that cleanliness at any rate is essential to it, and that this, if anything, divides him from the lower animals. So when we see one of

---

[2] Legendary son of Nestor, mentioned as a friend of Achilles.
[3] Charioteer of Achilles.

the other animals cleaning itself, we are wont to say in our surprise, "He does it like a man." And again, if some one finds fault with an animal for being dirty we are wont to say at once, as if in defense, "Of course he is not a man." So true is it that we think the quality to be distinctive of man, deriving it first from the gods. For since the gods are by nature pure and unalloyed, just in so far as men have approached them by virtue of reason, they have a tendency to purity and cleanliness. But since it is impossible for their nature to be entirely pure, being composed of such stuff as it is, the reason which they have received endeavors, so far as in it lies, to make this stuff clean.

The primary and fundamental purity is that of the soul, and so with impurity. You cannot find the same impurity in a soul as in a body: the soul's impurity you will find to be just this—that which renders it unclean for its own functions; and the functions of a soul are: impulse to act and not to act, will to get and will to avoid, preparation, design, assent. What is it then which renders the soul foul and unclean in these functions? It is nothing but its evil judgements. And so the soul's impurity consists in bad judgements, and purification consists in producing in it right judgements, and the pure soul is one which has right judgements, for this alone is proof against confusion and pollution in its functions.

And one ought to endeavor, as far as may be, to achieve a similar cleanliness in one's body too. Man's temperament is such that there must needs be mucous discharge: for this reason nature made hands, and the nostrils themselves like channels to cleanse his humours. If he swallows them I say that he does not act as a man should. It was impossible for men's feet not to be made muddy and dirty when they pass through mud and dirt; for this reason nature provided water and hands to wash with. It was impossible that some impurity should not stick to the teeth from eating. Therefore we are bidden to wash our teeth. Why? That you may be a man and not a beast or a pig. It was impossible that sweat and the pressure of our clothes should not leave some defilement clinging to the body, and needing to be cleansed. Therefore we have water, olive-oil, hands, towel, strigils, soap, and on occasion every other sort of apparatus, to make the body clean.

"Not for me," you say.

What! The smith will clean his iron tool of rust, and will have instruments made for the purpose, and even you will wash your plate when you are going to eat, unless you are absolutely foul and dirty, and yet you will not wash nor make clean your poor body? "Why should I?" says he. I will tell you again: first, that you may act like a man, next, that you may not annoy those you meet. You are doing something very like it even here, though you are not aware of it. You think you deserve to have a scent of your own. Very well, deserve it: but do you think those who sit by you deserve it too, and those who recline by you, and those who kiss you? Go away then into a wilderness, where you deserve to go, and live by yourself, and have your smell to yourself, for it is right that you should enjoy your uncleanness by yourself. But if you are in a city, what sort of man are you making yourself, to behave so thoughtlessly and inconsiderately? If nature had trusted a horse to your care, would you have left it uncared for? Imagine that your body has been committed to you as a horse: wash it, rub it down well, make it such that no one will shun it or turn from it. But who does not turn from a man who is dirty, odorous, foul-complexioned, more than from one who is bespattered with muck? The smell of the latter is external and accidental, that of the former comes from want of tendance; it is from within, and shows a sort of inward rottenness.

"But Socrates rarely washed."

Why, his body was clean and bright, nay, it was so gracious and agreeable that the handsomest and noblest were in love with him, and desired to recline by him rather than by those who were perfect in beauty. He might have never washed or bathed, if he had liked: I tell you his ablutions, if rare, were powerful. If you will not wash in hot water, wash in cold.

But Aristophanes says:

> *I mean the pallid folk, that shoeless go.*

True, but he also says he trod the air and stole clothes from the Gymnasium. The fact is, that all who have written about Socrates bear witness to just the opposite: he was not only pleasant to hear, but pleasant to look upon. They write the same again about Diogenes.

You must not scare away the masses from philosophy by your bodily appearance, but show yourself cheerful and unruffled in the body as in other things. "Men, look at me, I have nothing, I need nothing; without house, without city, an exile, if it so chance, and without a hearth, behold how I live a life more tranquil and happy than all the noble and the rich: but you see also that my poor body is not disfigured by my hard living!" But if a man says this to me, and wears the face and figure of one condemned, no god will ever persuade me to come near philosophy, if that is the sort of men she makes. Far be it from me: though it were to make me wise, I would not.

By the gods, when the young man feels the first stirrings of philosophy I would rather he came to me with his hair sleek than dishevelled and dirty: for that shows a sort of reflection of the beautiful, and a longing for the comely, and where he imagines these to be, there he spends his effort. It only remains then to point him the way and say, "Young man, you are in search of the beautiful, and you do well. Know then, that it is to be found where your reason is. Seek for it in the region of impulses to act and not to act, in the region of the will to get and the will to avoid. This is your distinctive possession, your body is born to be but clay. Why do you toil for it in vain? Time, if nothing else, will teach you that it is nothing." But if he comes to me befouled, dirty, with a beard trailing to his knees, what can I say to him, what similitude can I use to attract him? To what is he devoted that has any likeness to the beautiful, that I may change his direction and say, "The beautiful is not here, but here"? Would you have me say to him, "The beautiful is to be found not in filthiness but in reason"? Does he want the beautiful? Does he show any sign of it? Go and reason with a pig, that he wallow no more in the mire! That was why Xenocrates'[1] discourses laid hold on Polemo, for he was a young man of taste; he had come with glimmerings of devotion to the beautiful, though he sought it elsewhere.

Why, nature did not make even those lower animals dirty who associate with men. Does a horse or a well-bred dog wallow in mire? No, it is only the pig, and greasy geese, and worms and spiders, creatures the furthest removed from human society. Do you then, being a man, choose to be a wretched worm or spider, lower even than the animals that associate with men? Will you never wash, be it how you will? Will you not cleanse yourself? Will you not come clean among us that you may give pleasure to your companions? What! do you enter our temples, where custom forbids spitting or wiping the nose, in this condition, a man of filth and drivel?

"What?" you ask. "Do you call on us to adorn ourselves?"

Far from it, if it be not with our natural adornment of reason, judgements, activities, and the body only so far as to be cleanly and give no offence. If you hear that you must not wear scarlet, must you needs go off and spread filth on your cloak, or tear it in half?

"But how am I to have a beautiful cloak?"

Man, you have water, wash it. Here is a young man worthy to be loved, here is an old man worthy to love and to be loved, one to whom a man is to hand over his son to be instructed: daughters and young men will come to him, if it so chance, and for what? That he may discourse to them on a dunghill? God forbid. All eccentricity springs from some human source, but this comes near to being inhuman altogether.

---

[1] Xenocrates of Chalcedon, a Platonist and for twenty-five years head of the Academy (396–314 B.C.).

CHAPTER 12: On Attention

When you relax your attention for a little, do not imagine that you will recover it wherever you wish, but bear this well in mind, that your error of today must of necessity put you in a worse position for other occasions. For in the first place—and this is the most serious thing—a habit of inattention is formed, and next a habit of deferring attention: and you get into the way of putting off from one time to another the tranquil and becoming life, the state and behavior which nature prescribes. Now if such postponement of attention is profitable, it would be still more profitable to abandon it altogether: but if it is not profitable, why do you not keep up your attention continuously?

"I want to play today."

What prevents you, if you attend?

"I want to sing."

What prevents you, if you attend? Is any part of life excluded, on which attention has no bearing, any that you will make worse by attention, and better by inattention? Nay, is there anything in life generally which is done better by those who do not attend? Does the carpenter by inattention do his work better? Does the helmsman by inattention steer more safely? and is any of the minor duties of life fulfilled better by inattention? Do you not realize, that when once you have let your mind go wandering, you lose the power to recall it, to bring it to bear on what is seemly, self-respecting, and modest: you do anything that occurs to you and follow your inclinations?

To what then must I attend? First to those universal principles I have spoken of: these you must keep at command, and without them neither sleep nor rise, drink nor eat nor deal with men: the principle that no one can control another's will, and that the will alone is the sphere of good and evil. No one then has power to procure me good or to involve me in evil, but I myself alone have authority over myself in these matters. So, when I have made these secure, what need have I to be disturbed about outward things? What need have I to fear tyrant, or disease, or poverty, or disaster?

"But I do not please So-and-so."

Well, is he my doing? Is he my judgement?

"No."

What concern is it of mine then?

"Nay, but he is highly thought of."

That will be for him to consider, and for those who think much of him: I have One Whom I must please, One to Whom I must submit myself and obey—God and those who come next to God. He commended me to myself, and made my will subject to me alone, and gave me rules for the right use of it; and if I follow these in syllogisms I pay no heed to any one who contradicts me, if I follow them in dealing with variable premisses I pay regard to no one. Why then am I annoyed by those who criticize me in greater matters? What is the reason for this perturbation? It is none other than that I have had no training in this sphere. For every science is entitled to despise ignorance and the ignorant, and this is true of arts as well as of sciences. Take any shoemaker, any carpenter you like, and you find he laughs the multitude to scorn when his own craft is in question.

First then we must have these principles ready to our hand. Without them we must do nothing. We must set our mind on this object: pursue nothing that is outside us, nothing that is not our own, even as He that is mighty has ordained: pursuing what lies within our will, and all else only so far as it is given us to do so. Further, we must remember who we are, and by what name we are called, and must try to direct our acts to fit each situation and its possibilities.

We must consider what is the time for singing, what the time for play, and in whose presence: what will be unsuited to the occasion; whether our companions are to despise us, or we to despise ourselves: when to jest, and whom to mock at: and on what occasion to be conciliatory and to whom: in a word, how one ought to maintain one's character in society. Wherever you swerve from any of these principles, you suffer loss at once; not loss from without, but issuing from the very act itself.

What then? Is it possible to escape error altogether? No, it is impossible: but it is possible to set one's mind continuously on avoiding error. For it is well worth while to persist in this endeavor, if in the end we escape a few errors, and no more. As it is, you say, "I will fix my attention tomorrow": which means, let me tell you, "Today I will be shameless, inopportune, abject: others shall have power to vex me: today I will harbor anger and envy." Look what evils you allow yourself. Nay, if it is well to fix my attention tomorrow, how much better to do so today! If it is profitable tomorrow, much more so is it today: that you may be able to do the same tomorrow, and not put off again to the day after.

CHAPTER 13: To Those Who Lightly Communicate Their Secrets

When a man seems to have talked frankly to us about his own affairs, how we are drawn to communicate our own secrets to him and think this is frankness! First because it seems unfair to have heard our neighbor's affairs and yet not give him a share of our own in turn: next because we think we shall not give the impression of being frank if we are silent about our own affairs. In fact we often find men in the habit of saying, "I've told you all my affairs, won't you tell me any of yours? How is that?" Besides we think we may safely confide in one who has already confided his affairs to us: for we have a sort of feeling that he would never talk of our affairs for fear that we should talk of his. This is exactly the way in which reckless persons are caught by soldiers in Rome. A soldier sits by you in civilian dress, and begins to speak ill of the Emperor: then, as you have, so to speak, taken security from him for his good faith in the fact that he began the abuse, you are led to speak your own mind and so are arrested and imprisoned. The same sort of thing happens to us in ordinary life. Still, though he has confided his affairs to me with security, am I to do the same to the first man I meet? No, I hear and hold my tongue, if I am that sort of man, but he goes off and tells every one. Then, if I hear what he has done, if I am like him, I go and tell his secrets, because I want to have my revenge, and so I bring confusion to others and myself.[1] But if I bear in mind, that one man does not harm another, but that it is his own acts which help or harm a man, I achieve this conquest—that I abstain from doing the same as he did, but still my own babbling has put me in the position I am in.[2]

"Yes," you say; "but it is unfair to hear your neighbor's secrets, and give him no share of your own in return."

Man, did I invite your confidences? Did you tell me your secrets on conditions, that you might hear mine in return? If you are a babbler and think every one you meet is a friend, do you want me to be like yourself? What! if you have done well to confide in me, but it is not possible to confide in you and do well, do you still want me to unbosom myself? That is just as though I had a sound cask and you an unsound one, and you came and handed over your wine to me to put it into my cask, and then were vexed that I did not trust my wine to you, because your cask had a hole in it.

What becomes of your equality now? You trusted to one who is trustworthy, self-respecting, who believes that good and harm depend on his own activities and on nothing outside: would you have me confide in you, you who have made light of your own will and want to get pelf or office or advancement at court, even at the cost of slaying your children like Medea? Where is the equality in that?

No, show yourself to me as one who is trustworthy, self-respecting, safe, show that your judgements are those of a friend, show that your vessel is not unsound, and then you will see that I will not wait for you

---

[1] This phrase, used also in II. 12, seems to be a colloquial expression for "making a muddle."
[2] *I.e.*, the position of having given away my secret.

to confide your affairs to me, but will come to you myself and ask you to hear mine. For who is there that will not use a goodly vessel, who that despises a loyal and faithful counsellor, who that will not gladly welcome one who is ready to share the burden of his distresses and to relieve him by the very fact of sharing in them?

"Yes; but I trust you, and you do not trust me."

In the first place you do not trust me; you are only garrulous and therefore cannot keep anything back. For if what you say is true, trust your secrets to me and no one else: instead of which, whenever you see any one at leisure, you sit down by him and say, "My brother, you are the dearest friend I have; I beg you to listen to my story." And you do this to those you have not known even for a short while. If you really trust me, you trust me, of course, because I am trustworthy and self-respecting, not because I told you my secrets. Let me too then be allowed to think as you do. Prove to me that if a man tells his secrets to another, he is therefore trustworthy and self-respecting. If that were so, I should have gone about the world telling every man my affairs, if that were going to make me trustworthy and self-respecting. It is not really so. No, to be trustworthy a man needs judgements beyond the ordinary. If you see that a man is devoted to things outside his own will and has made his will subject to these, be sure that he has countless persons who hinder and constrain him. He has no need of a pitch-plaster or a rack to make him reveal what he knows, but the nod of a pretty maid, if it so chance, will shake his principles, a kindness from one of Caesar's officers, a lust for office or inheritance, and countless other motives such as these. You must therefore remember generally, that confidences require trust and trustworthy principles: and where can you easily find these nowadays? Let me be shown a man who is so minded as to say, "I have no concern except with what is my own, with what is beyond hindrance and by nature free. This is the true good, and it is mine: all else I leave to the Giver of events to decide, and raise no question."